What others have to say about this book!

"Whatever your position about the conflict between Arab and Jew, Kuttab will make you re-think it." "A brilliantly even-handed assessment of what might work in Palestine/Israel." "Based on Kuttab's many years of first-hand involvement with what is happening on the ground." **Dr. John Quigley,** President's Club Professor of Law, Moritz College of Law, Ohio State University

☙

"It's great and an excellent contribution and push toward the conversation shifts that are emerging – yet still so lacking – in this moment. I look forward to seeing this booklet become an important part of the paradigm shifts we deeply need!" **Oriel Eisner**, Director, Center for Jewish Nonviolence

☙

"Wow, it's amazing. I am deeply impressed and absolutely encourage, even insist, that people read it. I am completely inspired by Jonathan Kuttab's clear, concise and much needed vision of the future grounded in the realities of history and the longings of both people for equity, dignity and security." **Rabbi Lynn Gottlieb**

☙

"This book is the start of a renewed conversation, a new frame, to end the current impasse which is causing so much suffering. It is for the reader to decide and to commit themselves to be part of real solutions to the conflict rather than irrelevant discussions about antiquated solutions." **Mubarak Awad**, Founder, Nonviolence International

"Jonathan Kuttab's *Beyond the Two-State Solution* is a treasured pathway to peaceful and just change. Kuttab is a Palestinian American who has listened carefully and responded deeply, giving all of us who have worked and prayed for the imprisoned on both sides of the crumbling Green Line a possibility of seizing together a Kairos moment. This carefully crafted monograph is a trail marker for real change and reduction of heart, soul, and physical suffering." **Thomas R. Getman**, past Director for International Relations, World Vision

"Thank you for the text of your terrific new book, which I read with deep interest and admiration. Your analysis and prescriptions are visionary and compelling, and could not be more timely. The book deserves wide circulation and attention. Drawing on your long and distinguished career as a Palestinian lawyer and activist, your book sets a new standard, not just for authoritative and careful analysis of the Israel-Palestine tragedy, but for its persuasive, accessible, and practical outline of the political requirements that could lead to a mutually acceptable peace. By addressing dispassionately the essential political, moral, cultural, and security issues of highest concern to both peoples, i.e. the right of return and refugees, land, settlements, and sovereignty, in your respect for the humanity of both peoples, your book is well designed to replace zero-sum fear and despair with a realistic vision of hope." **Ambassador Philip C. Wilcox**, former Chief of Mission and U.S. Consul General, Jerusalem.

Beyond the Two-State Solution

By Jonathan Kuttab

Nonviolence International
Washington, DC
2021

Nonviolence International

Copyright © 2021 by Nonviolence International

CC BY-NC-ND: This Creative Commons license allows reusers to copy and distribute the material in any medium or format in unadapted form only, for noncommercial purposes only, and only so long as attribution is given to the creator.

Kuttab, Jonathan
Beyond the Two-State Solution

The cover is designed by Slava Klimov.
The cover painting by Kamal Boullata, 1970s, oil on canvas, is held in a private collection.
Maps are courtesy of Amnesty International, and the Applied Research Institute – Jerusalem.

Printed in the United States of America.
ISBN: 9780984505609

.

Nonviolence International
https://www.nonviolenceinternational.net/

Table of Contents

1: Basic Conflict 1
2: The Grand Compromise 6
3: Settlements — the Fly in the Ointment 11
4: Collapse of the Grand Compromise 16
5: Three Attempts at Removing Settlers 26
6: The Oslo Process and the Trump Plan 34
7: Survival of the Language 37
8: Minimum Requirements 42
9: The Vision 48
10: Constitutional Guarantees 56
11: Objections and Challenges 60
12: False Democracy and the Demographic Demon 68
13: Unique Features 75
14: How to Get There 79
Executive Summary 89

1: Basic Conflict

The complex conflict in the Middle East, which fuels endless enmities and a "clash of civilization" between the East and West and underlies, or exacerbates numerous additional conflicts, can be boiled down to a major struggle between two mutually exclusive ideologies. Each ideology comes with its own narrative, long list of grievances, and a credible demand on the sympathies and resources of large populations and players from outside the region. These two are the Palestinian Arab Nationalist movement and the Jewish Zionist movement. Both movements developed and grew at roughly the same time and laid claim to the same land. They each demanded the support and sympathy of millions within and outside the region as they engaged in their struggles.

The Arab Nationalist movement in Palestine saw itself as a nationalist liberation struggle against foreign colonialists and occupiers. It saw itself as part of the Arab—and indeed part of the Third World anti-colonial struggle for liberation and self-determination. It had little knowledge of and no sympathy for the Zionist movement. It viewed Zionism only as an ally to and an extension of western colonialism, and indeed as a settler colonial movement encroaching on their homeland. It saw no legitimacy to the Zionist movement and viewed it as a mortal existential threat to itself and its homeland. Most Palestinians did not see Jews as a national entity, but as adherents to a venerated monotheistic religion. The connection of Jews to the Land was viewed as a hoax and a pretext. While Palestinians recognized that the Holy land is indeed sacred to Jews, Moslems and Christians, they viewed any political or national claim to their land as a colonial enterprise.

Any attempt by Zionists to establish a foothold in Palestine, through land purchases, Jewish immigration, or otherwise, was viewed with determined hostility. Even after the Holocaust in Europe, the massive influx of Jewish refugees into Palestine and their successful creation of the state of Israel, this continued to be the dominant Palestinian view.

The power of the new state with its massive victories and advances only re-enforced this. Palestinians continued to see Israel as an illegitimate enterprise lacking in any historical, moral, or legal justification. Israel was merely present as a hostile, invading, settler-colonial presence, established by the West at the expense of Palestinians on Palestinian land, and displacing the legitimate indigenous Palestinian population. Except for the small number of indigenous Palestinian Jews, who were viewed as Palestinians of the Jewish faith, the Palestinian nationalist movement recognized no other rights for Zionists or Jews in their homeland and yearned to reverse their displacement by these foreigners.

On the other hand, the Zionist movement developed in ignorance or total dismissal of the indigenous Arab population. Their movement was a European movement intended to create a Jewish state in Palestine and the gathering of Jews from all over the world into that state. Their slogan was "a land without a people for a people without a land." They developed their ideology for the ingathering of Jews into *Eretz Yisrael* based on historical ties, religious connection, and the necessity of finding a solution to European Christian antisemitism by creating a Jewish State in Palestine. They sometimes referred to this as the "liberation movement of the Jewish people" and spoke in terms of resisting British colonial rule but did not pay much attention to the existing indigenous Arab population. Those like Ze'ev Jabotinsky, who thought at all about the local population, knew it would be unreasonable to expect anything but resistance from them. He felt that only by convincing them of the futility of resistance through an iron wall of vastly superior military strength could there be any peace at all. To this day, many Zionists view the Arab nationalist movement as an extension of worldwide antisemitism. They see the presence and ideology of Palestinian nationalism as a threat to their very existence which must be resisted at all costs.

It is no wonder that the two movements clashed. Their awareness of each other was entirely antagonistic. Palestinian nationalism totally rejected Zionism and its claims and saw it as a mortal enemy and a continuing existential threat. Zionists on the other hand, dreamt of "spiriting away" the local population, and insisted on conflating it with the rest of the "Arab world". They wanted the Arab world to accept the new Jewish state and find a solution to Palestinian Arabs by absorbing them into their numerous states and leave Palestine to Jews. The ideology of Zionism had no room for Palestinian Arab nationalism or indeed for any Arabs in historic Palestine at all. Arabs may be "tolerated" as individuals, but only if they accepted that the state belonged to the Jews, and they were there as individuals and only on sufferance. The new state insisted that Jordan or some other Arab state represent their interest, and indeed for a long time refused to even use the word "Palestinian," insisting that they were an invented people, and that there is no such thing as Palestine or Palestinians.

The resistance of Palestinians to the Zionist project was often viewed as an extension of the antisemitism which led to the creation of the State of Israel in the first place. This provided an easy excuse (*security*) for expelling them, disenfranchising them, oppressing them, and sealing borders to deny their return to their homes and homeland. Under this view, the Land of Israel belongs only to the Jewish people whether by divine right, through a biblical promise to Abraham and his descendants, or through historical ties. Jews had been forcibly expelled from the Land two thousand years ago, and now were merely "returning" to their ancestral homeland. This "return" was enabled through existential necessity of worldwide persecution and antisemitism culminating in the Holocaust, or by virtue of the approval of superpowers and the United Nations. Whatever the basis for the claim, the goal was clear: create a Jewish state, as Jewish as France is French. The land would belong to the Jewish people and none others.

Without going into the merits of either position—and certainly without implying any symmetry, moral or otherwise between their claims—one thing is clear and true for both sides: they each developed their positions and created a narrative and reality which had no place for the other side within it. No Arab Palestinian leader saw any virtue or legitimacy in Zionism or the aspiration of Jews worldwide to be sovereign in Palestine, and no Zionist leader gave much thought to how Palestinian nationalism could live with or within *Eretz Yisrael*. The few Zionists who tried to do this were marginalized and their brand of Zionism dismissed. To the extent either side thought about the other, it was only as a threat to its very existence, which must be denied, ignored, delegitimized, demonized, expelled, or at the very least disenfranchised, subjugated, and dominated.

The creation of the state of Israel began with the expulsion of most of the Palestinians from their homeland, and the ingathering of Jewish immigrants from all over the world, which consolidated the Zionist position of the new state. These events only enforced and sharpened the clash between these two movements, with each calling on outsiders to support its desperate struggle for its very existence... Then came the war of 1967.

2: The Grand Compromise

Much has been written about the 1967 War and the new situation it created. At the end of the war, Israel was left in control of the entire area of historic Palestine, as well as additional lands (the Sinai Peninsula from Egypt and the Golan Heights from Syria). But unlike the end of the war in 1948, Israel was also left with millions of Palestinian Arabs under its control. Initially, much energy went into each side blaming the other for starting that war. Israel claimed its action was a "preemptive self-defense" as the Arab armies were poised to attack it and that it never wanted to fight the war at all. Israel proclaimed that it had no territorial ambitions whatsoever, but that now that it was in a commanding position, it would never return to a vulnerable position. It was only holding onto the lands it captured as bargaining chips. It would insist on full recognition, security arrangements and peaceful relations with the Arab world before it would return the territories that had come into its possession during that war. On the other hand, Arabs referred to the war as the June Aggression. They vowed to "erase the results of the aggression" and proclaimed that they would never accept its results. After meeting in an Arab Summit in Khartoum, Arab leaders loudly declared: No Recognition, No Negotiations, No Peace.

Palestinians, who had placed so much hope and faith in Pan-Arabism and the support of the Arab nations, were most distressed. They decided that they needed to take matters into their own hands, and that they must now assert their specific national claim as Palestinians and resort to armed struggle to obtain their rights and liberate their lands rather than wait on the Arabs to do it for them. The Palestine Liberation Organization (PLO)—which had originally been created by the Arab League under Ahmad Shuqairi as a tool for Pan Arab nationalism—now reorganized itself under the leadership of Yasser Arafat. It demanded to be recognized as the true representative of the Palestinian People, rather than a weak adjunct of the Arab League. It also began a campaign of armed resistance to achieve its objectives.

On the international scene, however, a new reality had been created by the Israeli victory. Gradually, and after many fits and starts, the outlines of a possible Grand Compromise between these two movements began to take shape: Israel would return the land it captured in that war, and in return, the Palestinians and the Arab world would acknowledge Israel's sovereignty over the 78% of Palestine that constituted the State of Israel on the eve of that war. They would grant Israel legitimacy, recognition, and normalcy and end the state of war and belligerency. This Grand Compromise, often referred to as "Land for Peace" was enshrined in UN Resolution 242, and later strengthened by Resolution 338. That resolution included a reference to a just resolution of the Palestinian refugee problem by acknowledging their right to return or else accept compensation. Initially, Palestinians and many Arabs rejected this formula, but gradually, it obtained the support of solid majorities both among Palestinians and Arabs, as well as Israelis and their supporters abroad. The Two-State Solution became the acknowledged goal for all well-meaning people and individuals as the ideal formula for a peaceful solution of the Arab-Israeli conflict. Those who rejected it from either side, were viewed as maximalist hardliners and enemies to peace.

To be sure, there were detractors on both sides who rejected this solution and worked tirelessly to undermine it. They continued to assert their maximalist ideologies, but sometimes paid lip service to the two-state solution, often blaming the other side for failing to implement it. Gradually, however, two-state solution became the "only game in town." Even those who rejected its main tenets and fundamental presuppositions found it far easier to hide their true colors and pay lip service to the two-state solution while continuing on their agenda. One tactic was to add toxic conditions and elements at the right moment to ensure that the other side backed away before they were forced to act positively towards making that solution a reality.

Several elements appeared to be fundamental to the two-state solution:

Security Arrangements. From Israel's point of view, the pre-1967 borders were too vulnerable. They had a list of specific requirements to ensure long-term security, once they withdrew from the Occupied Territories. These arrangements were never fully articulated, but they included (i) keeping the new Palestinian state essentially demilitarized; (ii) some presence, or at least early-warning and monitoring posts along the Jordan river, which would be manned by and perhaps leased long-term to the Israeli army; (iii) some minimal border adjustments along the narrow Latrun salient which threatened to cut off Jerusalem from the rest of Israel; and (iv) security cooperation and coordination with the new Palestinian State to intercept and eliminate any potential attacks against Israel originating from the new state.

The Peace Treaty would be Final. This would be abandonment of Palestinian Arab claims to the original state of Israel (78% of historic Palestine), and ending the state of belligerency. The two-state solution required entering into genuine forms of cooperation and mutually beneficial relations at all levels between the two communities and the larger Arab and Moslem worlds. There was to be a clear understanding that the peace treaty is final, and not merely an interim step with more Palestinian claims to follow.

No Palestinian Right of Return. Palestinians would abandon their Right of Return to pre-1948 Israel. The problem of Palestinian refugees would be solved outside the boundaries of the State of Israel except for a minimal symbolic number (100,000 over ten years was sometimes mentioned). Thus, the Right of Return would be restricted to the new state of Palestine which would be created in the territories from which Israel would withdraw.

Cooperation. Cooperation and the establishment of a mutually beneficial relationship between the new state of Palestine and Israel would occur.

Jerusalem, the Capital of Two States. The Holy City of Jerusalem would be shared in a manner that recognized the historic and religious rights of both communities to the Holy City, including the acceptance of its unique status and allowing it to be the capital of both states.

Many ordinary Israelis felt that since they physically controlled the land, they were the ones making tangible compromises, and only getting intangible "promises" from the other side. They reluctantly agreed to two-state solution as the minimum "floor" of what they would accept. From the Palestinian side, the two-state solution was viewed as the "ceiling" of what they would tolerate. It was a huge compromise and derogation of their national claims, which could only be tolerated if the new Palestinian state was to be truly sovereign in all aspects (except for being demilitarized and sharing Jerusalem). Any additional derogation was viewed as totally undermining the essence of the compromise and making it no longer reasonable. Nonetheless, people of goodwill within both communities as well as others both in the region and in the outside world felt that this compromise made a lot of sense. It was to be pursued assiduously as the only real pragmatic solution possible. Consecutive American administrations in particular, spent much energy into making this solution a reality, and the Oslo Process was undertaken precisely to create the necessary trust and begin the process leading to such a resolution.

3: Settlements – the Fly in the Ointment

As soon as the guns were silent in 1967, the issue of Jewish settlements in the newly occupied territories became a central and defining feature of the conflict between Zionism and Palestinian nationalism: For Zionist ideologues, drunk with the power of their recent smashing victory, and realizing the utter weakness of the Arabs, this was the golden opportunity to realize the full potential of their Zionist dream. The entire land was now in Israel's possession. They had the physical power, control, legislative instruments and the ability to implement their goal and make the rest of historic Palestine ("Judea and Samaria" and Gaza) an integral part of the Jewish state of Israel. The Arabs who continued to live there were indeed a problem, but they were defeated and ill-equipped to prevent this scheme. They were immediately placed under military rule. A regime was established that made every aspect of their lives subject to permits and licenses which the army and its civil administration totally controlled. Soon, Israeli Jews were jubilantly travelling throughout the newly occupied territories and learning to love it as part of their patrimony.

The Israeli government, however, could not move too conspicuously in that direction as it needed to take into account international law and public opinion. International law neither allowed annexation nor the demographic shifts required to fulfill the Zionist ideal in terms of ejecting the non-Jewish population and moving Jews into the newly occupied territories. All such Zionist activity, therefore, needed to be carefully camouflaged and justified in secular non-Zionist terms. It had to be justified either as a security measure, temporary arrangement, or the creation of bargaining chips for the peace negotiations that were to come.

After all, Israel was loudly maintaining that it had no territorial ambitions, and only started the war in 1967 as a preemptive defensive measure.

For Palestinians and other Arabs, the 1967 war was only a continuation of the 1948 Nakba. Palestinians who happened to be out of the area at the end of the war, or who left as a result of the war were promptly blocked from returning. Israel started taking property all over the West Bank and Gaza under a variety of excuses and legal machinations and making that land available for Jewish settlers. Jewish settlers started moving in and creating exclusive Jewish enclaves which gave every indication of permanence. It is noteworthy that these settlements were not *Israeli* per se (Israeli Arab citizens were barred from them) but specifically and exclusively *Jewish*.

For Palestinians this settlement enterprise was in fact the heart and essence of the conflict, to be gained, or lost, one dunum and one soul at a time. But to properly frame and wage their struggle, Palestinians first needed to get Arab recognition of their right to speak in their own voice, as Palestinians and not just as "Arabs" whose rights were championed by Jordan or Egypt. Only then could they advance their struggle which their Arab brethren had so far failed to do.

Israeli settlers felt they were true pioneers and true Zionists. They set up their exclusive Jewish settlements using the authority of the Israeli army and its resources. At the same time, they did not feel that they needed to be restrained by whatever political considerations the government may have had. The Israeli government, therefore, found it necessary to play a duplicitous role: On the one hand, it loudly proclaimed that settlement activity was temporary and part of the necessities of a belligerent occupation. It publicly proclaimed that it was eager for a solution whereby the land and settlements would be traded for a lasting peace. At the same time, the government was providing all forms of logistical assistance, infrastructure, land acquisition, and construction as well as inducements to promote the settlements. The actual progress of the settlements reflected the policies of the consecutive Israeli governments and their separate assessments of their ability to hang on to the territories in the future. But each administration participated massively in the settlement program and in the cover up of their true intentions towards keeping the territories.

The ideological Zionists, realizing this dichotomy between stated positions and true intentions of the government felt it was their duty to "push the envelope" and act outside the stated parameters. They knew full well that the Israeli government would back them in their immediate needs and would eventually "legalize" the settlements in the future. They wholeheartedly embraced the Israeli saying, "What matters is not what the *goyyim* (Gentiles) say, but what the Jews do." The government was understandably reluctant to set up Jewish settlements in the heart of the densely populated Arab Centers, such as Hebron, but once the "visionaries" started a settlement, the government would almost inevitably relent. It would provide each settlement with protection, infrastructure, water, electricity, roads, and additional land for expansion (taken from the Arabs), and eventually formal recognition. The debate in Israel between the Left and the Right, more often than not centered on tactics and what would or would not be allowed by the international community, and particularly the United States. Rarely did the Left challenge the ideological basis for the settlement activities in terms of Zionism and the "right" of Jews to take possession of and settle in the land.

The story of the "creeping annexation" and the dual position of the consecutive Israeli governments is a fascinating and instructive story. Much can be said about what was wrong with settlements in general, but the public debate in Israel centered on *which* settlements should be built, and *where*, and what reasons or excuses could be made for them. For our purposes, the most crucial thing about settlements is that they totally, fully, and radically contradicted and undermined the possibility of a two-state solution. To be sure there were many objections to settlements. They constituted land theft of both private and communal land; they were illegal under Geneva IV; and they required an apartheid system where two populations coexist side by side under vastly different legal, economic, and political systems. From a Jewish point of view, there were also objections to the moral or ethical basis for settlements, which recalled the shadow of ghettoization. The major objection, however, was that any credible two-state solution required an "Arab" Palestine in 22% of historic Palestine, in return for abandoning Palestinian claims in Israel as it existed before the 1967 war. In this sense, settlements became the primary impediments for a two-state solution, and those dedicated to it necessarily saw the settlers as the spoilers of any possibility of implementing the Grand Compromise.

To those Jewish Israelis who were not committed to the two-state solution, however, the position of the settlers was not only understandable, but a more coherent, principled manifestation of Zionism and the aspirations of its adherents. To them it was difficult to explain why Jews can claim a right to Haifa and Jaffa, but not to Hebron, the city of the Patriarchs, or East Jerusalem, where the sacred Temple once stood. It was also difficult to show why Jews should be prohibited from living or settling anywhere in historic Palestine. At the same time, settlers saw no reason to abandon any of their economic, social, health, educational, services or rights as Israelis. Neither did they relish the prospect of submitting to the rules that govern those whom they had defeated, much less to allow themselves to be ruled by them in any future peace agreement.

In fact, any hint that peace was approaching, or an agreement was about to be achieved, sent panic through the settler community and led to a renewed effort to grab more land. It is no wonder that the very mention of a two-state solution was anathema in settler circles since it was viewed correctly as requiring a reversal of their entire enterprise. When Prime Minister Netanyahu was pressured to publicly state that he supported a two-state solution position (which was the official declared position of the government) he did so with great reluctance and risked paying a political price for it. Pro-settlement activists even worked to have the words "Two State Solution" removed from the political platform of the US Democratic Party in 2016.

4: Collapse of the Grand Compromise

*"All the King's Soldiers
All the King's Men
Couldn't Put Humpty
Together Again."*

From the beginning, the goal of the settlement enterprise was to create "facts on the ground" that would be difficult, if not impossible, to change at a later time. For example, some of the most immediate activities in the settlement realm were started as early as 1967 and centered on East Jerusalem. The entire Moghrabi Quarter in the Old City was razed to create a plaza in front of the Western Wall, and two rings of residential high-rise settlements were created in East Jerusalem, cutting it off from the rest of the West Bank. This policy eventually led to introducing enough Jews into the expanded East Jerusalem to create a Jewish majority there, thus making East Jerusalem a permanent part of the State of Israel. East Jerusalem was also subjected to a special regime that differed from the rest of the West Bank. The success of that policy was such that most Israelis today do not think of these settlements as part of the "issue of settlements" but consider them as normal Jewish neighborhoods in a united Jerusalem. This is even true of many on the Left whose opposition to settlements and settlement activities does not include opposition to the settlements in East Jerusalem.

Additional activities were undertaken in the rest of the occupied territories to create Jewish settlements there, complete with their own infrastructure and even a separate road system connecting them with each other and with Israel. These activities were in line with Zionist ideology that would eventually create irreversible new facts on the ground and preclude a two-state solution.

Today, over fifty years after the 1967 war, it seems clear to any objective observer that the "facts on the ground" that were created have reached a level of solidity and permanence that makes them impossible to reverse. This simple fact, which is well understood and acknowledged in Israel and Palestine, nonetheless needs to be more clearly delineated since it runs contrary to the "two state" language and logic which permeates and even monopolizes the discussion internationally.

Settlements are an Irreversible Fact
Here is why I think the Jewish settlements have indeed become an irreversible fact, making the two-state solution impossible:

Sheer Numbers. Today there are over 700,000 Jewish settlers who have moved into the occupied territories and made their homes there. They live in coherent communities, with homes, playgrounds, gardens, graveyards, swimming pools, neighbors, schools, a University, infrastructure, and all the fabric of civilian life. They are "at home" there as much as any Jewish Israeli is within the Green Line (the 1967 border). To even contemplate uprooting them at this time is to contemplate a major emotional and humanitarian disaster of monumental proportions. It is true that their presence was illegal in the first place and that they are actually living on stolen property. It is also true that the very structure of their communities is racist, discriminatory and exclusivist, being closed also to non-Jewish Israeli citizens. Furthermore, there is an international consensus on the illegality of these settlements.

However, all these factors are beside the point. To uproot them now would be so disruptive of the lives of the settlers, their children, and the entire fabric of Jewish Israeli society that it is difficult to contemplate. If an Israeli government were to attempt it, the effect would be so disruptive that it may well plunge the country into civil war. Whether such an outcome can be obtained by bribery (compensation), fear or compulsion, there is no question as to its enormous cost in human terms alone, and that the political will to do it is beyond the capability of any Israeli government. The fact that tens of thousands of these settlers are also fundamentalists who have dedicated their lives to the settlement enterprise will further ensure that removing them could not be accomplished without starting a civil war. Settlers today constitute about ten percent of the Jewish population of Israel, and they are well organized to resist any attempt to remove them.

Location. Some early efforts were made by different Israeli governments to plan the location of settlements strategically in order to achieve specific military or geopolitical goals. However, the reality on the ground is that settlements have been created throughout the occupied territories, sometimes haphazardly, as the opportunity arose. Often, the settlements were created as small horseshoe shaped dots on a map, with the goal of closing up and swallowing up the lands in between. They were usually started on a hilltop, gradually expanding downhill to take up more land on the slopes.

At one point, then-Israeli Minister of Agriculture Ariel Sharon, fearing that a peace agreement was near, publicly encouraged settlement youth to take the initiative and capture hilltops without waiting for government approval anywhere in the West Bank. He said that this way, settlements would have commanding positions to claim more and more lands on the sides of the hilltops in any future peace arrangement. The term "hilltop youth" was coined for the largely unruly and mostly youthful fanatical settlers who took up this call. These youth would forcibly establish "outposts" without government permission or direction, sometimes even in the face of government opposition. This they would do with the knowledge that eventually their outposts would be retroactively supported, expanded and legitimized by subsequent actions of the government.

A recent study by the organization Peace Now outlined the precise mechanisms used by different government agencies to support and enable over ninety "illegal" outposts that were (and still are) contrary to Israeli law and public policy.

Subsequent efforts by Israeli governments attempted to bring some cohesion into these outposts and bunch most of them into "settlement blocks" for which grand plans were later created to encompass and regulate them. Nonetheless, the more radical settlers felt that they were the true Zionists and that they could act with impunity. They ignored stated government policies, knowing they would be eventually vindicated. The fact that they often took private Palestinian land—for which the convoluted legal cover used to justify such land theft had not been completed—was irrelevant to them.

As stated before, in certain cases the declared intent of the government for some settlements, was to locate them in such a manner as to block the possibility of a future Palestinian state. At other times, the Israeli government would insist that such offending settlements were not authorized or legitimate and would be removed in an eventual peace agreement. Regardless, the result is that the location of settlements has become an additional factor which makes it impossible to establish a coherent and contiguous Palestinian state in the West Bank.

Road Network. The Israeli settlements, whether officially sanctioned by the Israeli government or not, were connected to each other and to the state of Israel by a network of modern roads. These roads enabled the settlers to have fast access to work, or cultural and other centers in Israel. Such roads were segregated and dedicated for the sole exclusive use of Jewish settlers. The fact that such roads often further fragmented and inconvenienced Palestinian residential areas was not a worry to Israel. Where the roads bordered upon Palestinian villages or towns, physical objects, such as cement blocks or iron gates were placed to prevent Palestinian villagers from accessing or benefitting from them.

Sometimes high walls surrounded such roads, blocking from view the Palestinian villages they bordered. These roads sometimes followed the route of original West Bank roads which now could no longer be used by Palestinians, who were forced to make do with other roundabout roads to reach their destinations. Shimon Peres once actually embarked on a fundraising effort to urge the Europeans to donate fifty million USD to provide the hapless Palestinians with alternative roads. Settler roads often cut off a village from its agricultural lands. Access to such lands, if at all possible, was done by travelling long distances and using gates that were not always open or available to the farmers. The land for each of these roads (together with swaths of land on both sides) was taken from Palestinians under public domain even though the roads only benefited Jewish settlers.

As these roads were built, they increasingly cut off Palestinian Arab communities from each other. When pushed by one American administration on this very point (that a viable contiguous Palestinian state could not possibly exist given the settlements and their locations) Israeli politicians had a creative answer: "transportation contiguity." Palestinian areas could be connected through tunnels and bridges creating a "transportation contiguity" even though the area left for Palestinians more closely resembles Swiss cheese than any recognizable shape. One such bridge/tunnel near the village of Hizma was in fact constructed, allowing transportation contact between Palestinian areas under the fast highway connecting settlements to Israel, but this tunnel was soon blocked with boulders and dirt and remains closed today.

Infrastructure of Governance. In addition to the physical structures, an entire administrative system of governance was legislated through military orders. These regulations organized the settlement areas into "Regional Councils" with an elaborate structure of court, police, services, electricity, water grids, and mobile phone connections. It also included a localized paramilitary system of local security for the Jewish settlers (parallel, but distinct from the Israeli Army units). Every attempt was made to provide the Jewish inhabitants with all the advantages and amenities of Israeli citizens, while their homes and communities were also heavily subsidized. The settlements were given added tax exemptions and privileges as "development towns"—a status never granted to Arab Palestinian towns within Israel itself.

Initially, the settlements appeared as isolated dots on the Palestinian map of the West Bank. Today, most of the West Bank is composed primarily of Jewish regional councils with isolated and restricted Palestinian enclaves in their midst. Much of the open space between Arab villages and towns is now officially designated as Area C (which accounts for about sixty percent of the West Bank area) and is under the direct control of the Israeli Civil Administration. Practically no Arab building or development is allowed there. Prime Minister Netanyahu promised his voters that he would annex and claim full Israeli sovereignty over all Area C land. A few years ago, settlers protested that a water pipe leading to the only new Palestinian town in the West Bank (Rawabi) "infringed upon their territory" by passing a few hundred meters into Area C. While in theory Area C is under the control of the Civil Administration of the Israeli Army, and the Palestinian Authority has no jurisdiction there, the settlers have treated all of Area C as "theirs" and even call for its formal annexation into Israel.

Psychological Integration. Israelis both in and out of the government treat the settlements as an integral part of Israel. The soccer teams of the settlements are part of the Israeli national league. Israelis treat any attempt to distinguish between the settlements and Israel as crass discrimination. New laws even prohibit making such distinctions or distinguishing the products of the settlements from Israeli products. Israelis under the age of seventy-three have known no reality in their adult lives where the settlements and the "Territories" were not under Israeli control. Israeli maps do not show the "Green Line" at all. Despite international law and the understanding of the rest of the world, for Israelis, the "occupied territories" are not in fact "occupied" but part of their homeland.

To give up any part of the occupied territories, especially the populated settlements, would be a traumatic experience for Israelis.

It would be viewed as a net loss, and a concrete tangible compromise in return for intangibles such as "recognition" or "peace." In all cases, it remains very difficult to justify in ideological Zionist terms. Many soldiers in uniform have openly stated they will not participate in evacuating Jews from their homes in settlements even under direct orders. In this they have been supported by many public figures, rabbis, and even army officers.

The real effect of this psychological integration is to rule out any solution where the settlers would be abandoned to live under Palestinian rule or as part of a Palestinian state. Settlers think of themselves as proud Israelis and, if anything, more authentic Zionists than those living in the more secure coastal plain. To tell them that in order to stay in their homes they need to live under Palestinian law or be governed by the same rules and structures and public amenities and services applicable to West Bank Palestinians would be unthinkable. Settlements would have to be Israeli or nothing at all. In the meantime, settlements and settlers have been so thoroughly integrated into the fabric of Israeli society, that it is difficult for most Israelis to think of settlers as anything but Israeli.

LEGEND

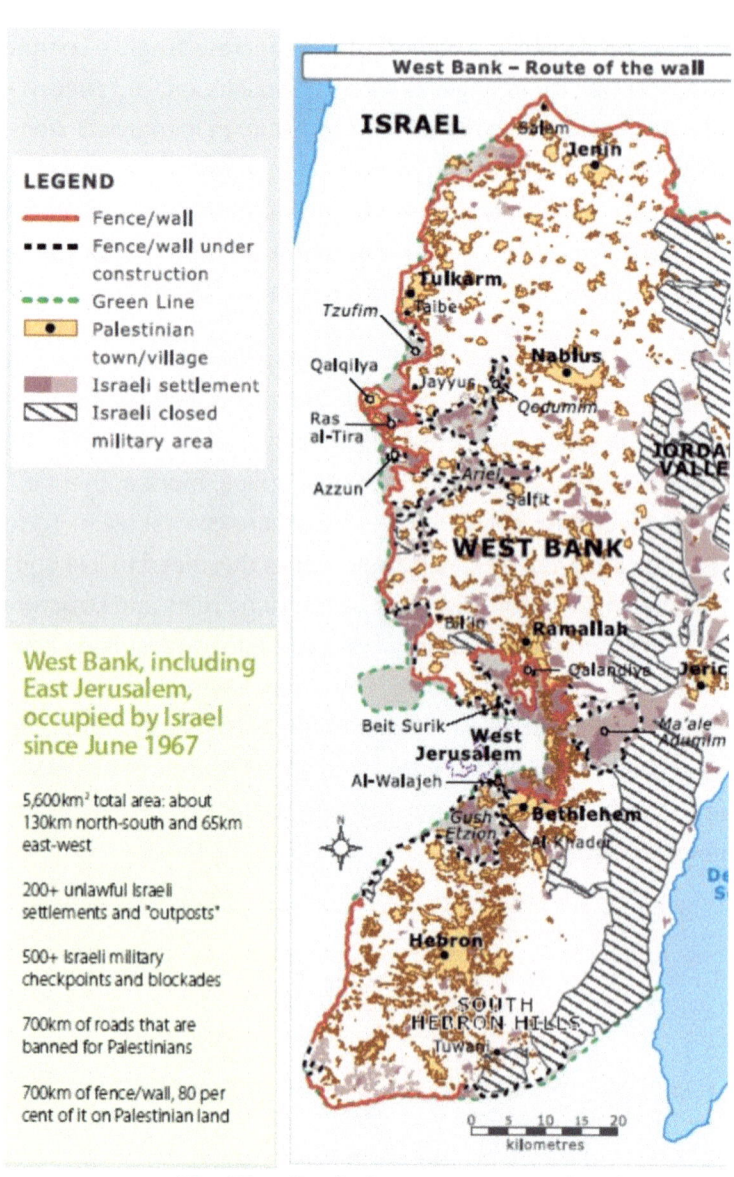

- ——— Fence/wall
- ■ ■ ■ ■ Fence/wall under construction
- ─ ─ ─ ─ Green Line
- ▣ Palestinian town/village
- ▰ Israeli settlement
- ▨ Israeli closed military area

West Bank, including East Jerusalem, occupied by Israel since June 1967

5,600km² total area: about 130km north-south and 65km east-west

200+ unlawful Israeli settlements and "outposts"

500+ Israeli military checkpoints and blockades

700km of roads that are banned for Palestinians

700km of fence/wall, 80 per cent of it on Palestinian land

The West Bank. Amnesty International

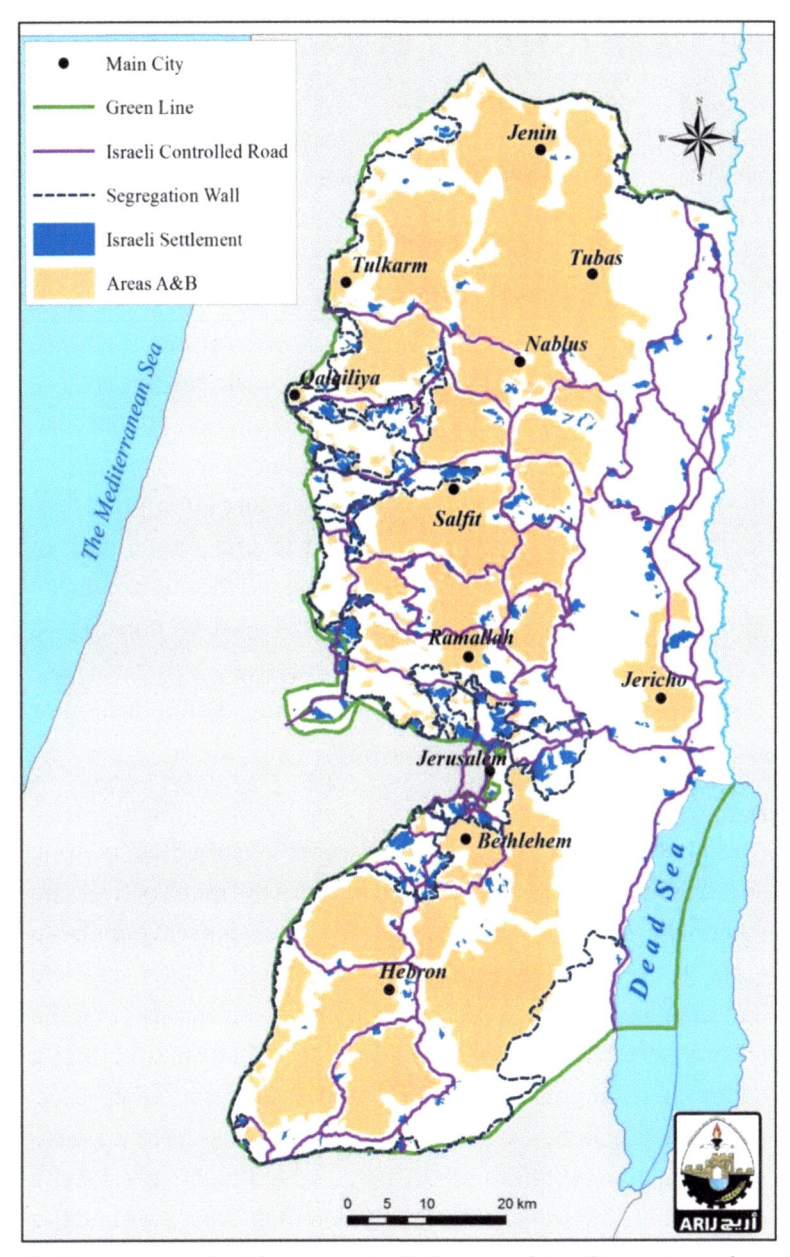

Settler roads and settlements. Applied Research Institute - Jerusalem

5: Three Attempts at Removing Settlers

As part of the Peace Treaty between Egypt and Israel, Israel evacuated and demolished the Yamit Salient settlements in Sinai, as it withdrew from the Sinai Peninsula and returned it to Egyptian sovereignty. President Sadat would not accept anything less as part of the Peace Agreement. In historic Palestine, there were three noteworthy attempts to remove Jewish settlers. Each was conducted after much hand wringing and public debate, and entirely as an intra-Israeli affair, without consultation or coordination with Palestinians. Each had a major effect psychologically on the Israeli public, potentially blocking any future attempts at "uprooting" Jewish settlers. It is important to understand each of these events in some detail to realize the practical impossibility of massive evacuations in the future. This must be done as we consider the question of whether the massive evacuations necessary for a two-state solution can be done, even if desired or required by legal or political necessity.

Gush Qatif Evacuations in Gaza
A total of seven thousand Jewish settlers inhabited twenty-one settlements in Gaza in 2005. They existed in the midst of over one million Palestinians living in one of the most densely populated areas in the world. Their settlements covered a large area and had to be guarded by over 3,000 soldiers. Even transporting the children to schools as well as the adults to and from Israel was a major logistical problem. It was carried out in armored vehicles, under heavy guard, and subject to frequent attacks. From a security point of view, these settlements were a nightmare for the Israeli army. The stark contrast between their living style and the surrounding abject poverty was both graphic and indefensible.

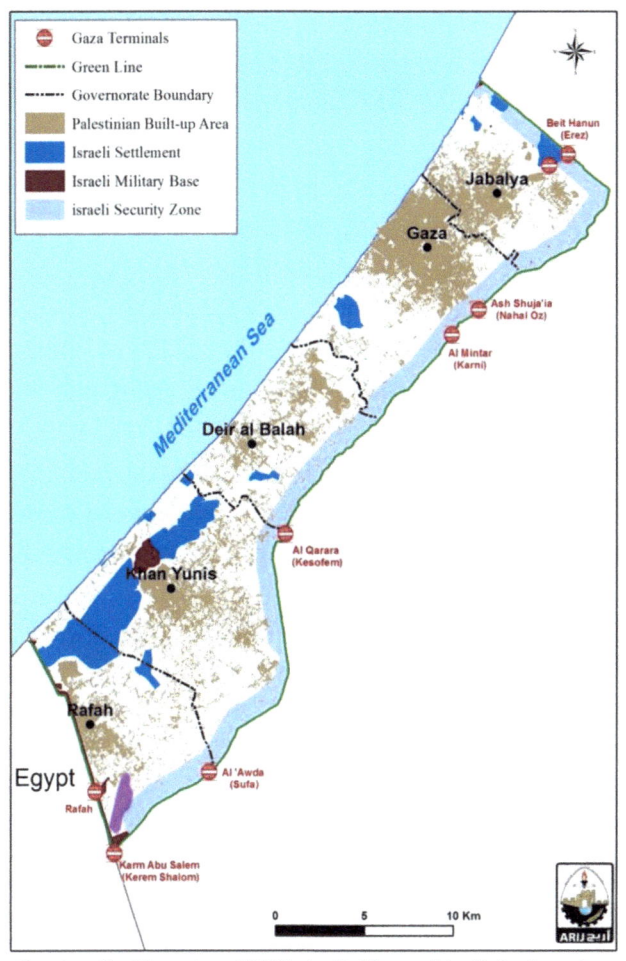

Gaza Israeli settlements until 2005. Applied Research Institute - Jerusalem

Ariel Sharon, then-defense minister, worked out a plan to unilaterally evacuate these settlements in return for obtaining ironclad assurances from the US. The US would accept "legitimizing and legalizing" settlement blocks in the West Bank. Israel could also claim that the "occupation of Gaza has ended" and obtain a free hand to besiege and attack Gaza almost at will. No coordination with the Palestinian Authority was sought, and no orderly transfer of the lands and fields of the settlements was arranged. Instead, the world was treated to a media circus as the settlers had to be forcibly evacuated and fought pitched battles with the Israeli army. Very generous compensation was given to the settlers, many of whom settled in the West Bank in new homes paid for by the Israeli government. Israel made much of the fact that the Palestinians scavenged and destroyed the evacuated settlements and their hothouses. In the Israeli mind, this showed both "painful concessions by Israel" and the futility of withdrawing settlements as it only invited "Palestinian aggression and savagery." In the current debate on settlements in Israel, this experience is often cited as a national trauma that should not be repeated. It is also used as a proof that settlements are not really the problem, and that removing them would not solve the conflict but only encourage Palestinian aggression and terrorism.

The Attempt to Evacuate Settlers from the Center of Hebron
In the midst of Hebron (population 180,000), extremist settlers set up three settlement points: One was Beit Hadassah, an old building that belonged to Jews in the 1920's. (This building was registered under the Jordanian Custodian of Enemy Property, and the Israeli Civil Administration, as its successor, took possession of it and gave it to Jewish settlers). The second was a public school (under the control of the Israeli Civil Administration, which evacuated the Palestinian students and turned the building over to the settlers). The third was the central bus station (clearly "public" property also controlled by the Civil Administration, which removed the buses to the outskirts of the city and turned the land over to settlers).

These three points, right in the very heart of a densely populated city became home to some of the most extreme Jewish settlers.

These settlers viewed their role as restoring the Jewish presence in Hebron by specifically harassing their Palestinian neighbors and forcing them to leave. They considered themselves a "nucleus" for the return of Jews to Hebron and made no attempt to hide their intention of removing the Arab population and restoring Hebron to Jewish hands. They would routinely spit on, hit, attack, and throw garbage and dirty water on passersby, constantly demanding army protection from any Palestinian who challenged or resisted their attacks. They even trained their children to do the same to Arab children, women, and the elderly. They became a major nuisance. Rabbi Moshe Levinger, one of those settlers, would often walk unarmed with Jewish children, insulting and harassing Palestinian Hebronites. The watchful adults (and soldiers) would wait for the slightest act of retaliation or attempts by the Arab victims to resist this provocation, in order to forcefully intervene on behalf of the settler children.

The army, which was called upon to provide the settlers with protection, had no authority to stop them or tell them what to do. These settlers were thought of as extreme even by the settlers in the nearby Kiryat Arba' settlement that was created on the outskirts of Hebron.

The absurdity of this situation came to a head in 1994, when one of the settlers, Baruch Goldstein, entered the Ibrahimi mosque and proceeded to massacre worshippers who were performing the dawn prayers at the mosque during Ramadan. Twenty-nine were killed, and one hundred and twenty-five wounded before the attacker himself was overcome and killed. Israeli soldiers at the site would later state that they had no authority to stop him or to intervene since they were army, and not police, and he was an Israeli civilian. The army would seize upon this later to establish a "blue" uniformed police outpost inside the mosque. The entire West Bank was in an uproar over this massacre, demanding revenge and international pressure mounted for some drastic action to be taken. The peace negotiations taking place at that time were suspended for months.

This seemed to be a perfect opportunity for Prime Minister Rabin, who was no friend of these extremists, to militarily evacuate the hundred or so families from the heart of the old city of Hebron for their own protection, if nothing else. It was well expected at the time that Hebron was to be turned over to the Palestinian Authority anyway, and the presence of these extremists in the very heart of Hebron made no sense whatsoever. Rabin said he was determined to evacuate them, and that if the settlers did not like it, they could "spin like propellers."

The settlers, however, would not leave. Instead, they created a campaign of immediate and intense pressure upon Rabin, with ministers threatening to resign and bring down the government. It was later claimed that some of the settlers had threatened to barricade themselves and that five of them would commit suicide if the army tried to evacuate them by force. "How could he possibly abandon the graves of the Patriarchs buried in Hebron and turn over authority there to non-Jews?" they demanded. "And how could he possibly justify prohibiting Jews from returning to and living in the ancient city of their ancestors, almost as holy to them, and full of historical significance as Jerusalem itself?"

In response to this political pressure Rabin, instead, imposed a curfew on the Arab population of Hebron, which lasted about forty-five days, while he tried to negotiate a consensual evacuation. International, US and Egyptian efforts were also enlisted to try to negotiate a reasonable compromise. In the end, he failed and the settlers prevailed. The main street (Alshuhada Street) was closed to Palestinian vehicular travel, and was divided down the middle, providing the settlers with a free corridor to reach Kiryat Arba by foot, while the Palestinian residents would use the other side of the street on foot, under heavy military guard. Settlers were granted additional increased security. Most of the shops on that street remained closed, and the center of the city gradually turned into a ghost town to this day. The political clout of settlers was demonstrated, when under these extreme circumstances, a "peace–oriented" Labor government was unable to evacuate even that small number of settlers from the heart of Hebron.

Evacuation of Amona
Amona is one of about ninety-four settler "outposts" that sprang up all over the West Bank. These outposts were not planned or officially sanctioned by any Israeli government, and seemed to spring up haphazardly, particularly on hilltops. Little effort was made to provide "justifications" for setting up the settlements. While the Israeli army provided protection, and different government entities provided assistance and infrastructure, the official position was that these settlements were illegal even under Israeli law. In many cases, as in Amona, the land involved was clearly private Palestinian land, and the convoluted methods for stripping ownership and claiming it to be "state land" or "absentee property" or "needed for security" or "public purposes" did not apply—and in this case were not even utilized.

In Amona, Palestinian private landowners waged a successful legal challenge, proving beyond doubt their private ownership and obtaining court orders in their favor. The High Court ordered the evacuation of the settlement outpost and the return of the land to its Arab owners. Despite convoluted arguments and extension after extension, the settlers refused to vacate, and the government was eventually forced to remove them. Intense political pressure, and threats to bring down the government led to generous offers of about a million shekels per person, and a promise to build a new settlement with over twice the number of residential units on another hill opposite to Amona.

Nonetheless, the drama continued, with all political parties—including the Left—showing tremendous understanding for the "plight" of the poor settlers who had to be uprooted. A day-long operation involving thousands of policemen, conducted pitched "battles" in which unarmed policemen politely and gently tolerated abuse and even attacks, while "persuading" frantic settlers and their supporters to allow the evacuation and enforcement of the court order to take place. The Jerusalem Mayor weighed in by dramatically increasing the number of demolitions of Arab homes built without license (whose licenses had been denied) within Jerusalem boundaries. The entire episode led to proposing a new Israeli law promising to retroactively "legalize" all ninety-four settlement outposts, even if built on private Arab land and without government approval or planning. The new Biden administration may change the tone, but it is unlikely to force substantive change on the ground.

Immovable Settlements Mean No Two-State Solution
Given these three attempts, it is little wonder that no one in Israel today seriously contemplates any substantial uprooting or removal of settlers in the West Bank. The declared position of the government was that with President Trump in power, there would be no more US pressure, and they could loosen what few

internal restraints still exist. Prime Minister Netanyahu publicly declared that he would not allow a single settler to be uprooted, and this promise he has kept. President Trump's "Deal of the Century" repeats this promise, that no settlers will be removed or evacuated from their homes. This means that the basic premise of the two-state solution cannot possibly be realized since a Palestinian state cannot exist without massive removal of Jewish settlers and dismantlement of a large number, if not all of the settlements.

It has been argued that the bulk of the settlements (the settlement blocks) can be allowed to remain and annexed to Israel through an agreement for land swaps, whereby Israel would grant a new Palestinian State equivalent land from Israel itself. However, even under the most optimistic scenarios, at least a hundred thousand settlers would still have to be removed to provide any serious coherent contiguous territory to such a state. As has been shown by the above three attempts, this is not a realistic possibility. The settlements and the settler outposts are so scattered throughout the West Bank, and so firmly rooted in Israeli psychology and political reality, that a contiguous Palestinian state is no longer physically possible.

6: The Oslo Process and the Trump Plan

In 1994, Israel and the Palestine Liberation Organization signed an Interim Agreement which established the Palestinian National Authority (PA) and started a tortured "peace process." The implicit understanding was that this process would eventually lead to a two-state solution. The authority of the PA was to be gradually expanded and the territory under its control increased until it matured into a full-blown Palestinian state. The hard issues of Jerusalem, the refugees, final borders, security arrangements, and settlements were left to be eventually addressed as "final status issues." Negotiations on these issues were to start in three years, and to be completed no later than five years after the signing of the original interim agreement.

Soon, however, the negotiations bogged down and eventually collapsed. Palestinians saw settlements continuing to expand, while Israelis demanded increasingly that the PA act in Israel's perceived interests, and not as an independent representative of its own people. After the assassination of Yitzhak Rabin, a new Israeli government under Benjamin Netanyahu (that was hostile to the Oslo Process to begin with) halted additional transfer of territory and powers to the PA. It also made additional increasing demands upon Palestinians and accelerated the settlement process. The rise of Hamas and its electoral success, and later takeover of internal affairs in Gaza gave Israel the excuse to cut off Gaza from the West Bank totally and impose a siege upon it. In many ways, the resulting situation became the best of all possible worlds for Israel's right-wing government. It had managed to pass the responsibility to the PA for managing the internal affairs of the majority of the West Bank population while yet retaining all the ultimate power and authority. The Palestinian leadership tried hard to pretend to be a real government while it lacked all authority to act as such, except against its own people.

Whether the parties had negotiated in good faith aiming towards a genuine two-state solution, or whether the process was flawed from the start, the result was the same. Settlements continued to expand and were solidified, this time with the apparent complicity and authorization of the Palestinian leadership. To show their commitment to peace and renunciation of "terrorism," the Palestinian Authority was required to stifle all forms of resistance by its own people and to forego all forms of their national struggle, including nonviolent forms. They were also required to abate any calls for international intervention. Diplomatic moves for recognition as a state or appeals to the world community and the International Criminal Court were viewed as violations of the Agreement, and as legitimate excuses for retaliation.

When the Trump Administration came into power, the right-wing settlers felt they could get US approval to formalize their victories and force Palestinians into a total capitulation. Trump's "Deal of the Century" had their fingerprints all over it. Unlike the Oslo Process, Trump's plan made little effort to hide its true intentions and proposed to give ideological Zionist maximalists everything they wanted. At the same time, it gave Palestinians "promises" of prosperity, but only if they met highly unreasonable conditions, to the satisfaction of Israel and the US. The five difficult "final status" issues were all resolved in Israel's favor: Jerusalem was to be recognized as exclusively Jewish and under its sole sovereignty. There was to be no Palestinian right of return; and the status of refugees was to be solved by the Arab states, absolving Israel of any responsibility in that regard. No settlers were to be removed at all, and Israel would be free to annex settlement blocks as it chooses. In regard to Israeli security, it would retain supreme authority over all the land, including in the areas under "Palestinian control." External borders and border crossings would be permanently under Israel's control, and internal "borders" would be drawn and determined by Israel and the United States.

The amazing thing is that the language of two-state solution was not totally abandoned. Instead it was specifically stated that statehood and sovereignty were "not exact terms, but their meaning could be determined by agreement of the parties." In other words, if Palestinians would agree and act in complete accordance with the "Deal of the Century" (to Israel's satisfaction), they would be allowed to call themselves a state, and to call certain neighborhoods outside the Wall "Jerusalem" or "Al Quds."

The fact that no Palestinians were found to accept this deal was immaterial. This was not to be a peace agreement between the two parties but a declaration of capitulation by Palestinians and total victory by the Zionist movement. Its pronouncement marked the official death of any meaningful two-state solution.

7: Survival of the Language

Despite the fact that almost every knowledgeable observer acknowledges privately that the two-state solution has no chance whatsoever, the language of two-state solution continues to predominate in discussions of Israel/Palestine. At best, pundits warn that "the window of opportunity is closing" and the "time for a two-state solution is running out."

Why is it that the language of two-state solution survives?

First: International Law
After 1967, the entire international community came to accept that despite whatever happened in 1948, the State of Israel, within its 1948 borders, was a fully integrated, recognized member of the international community. Despite previous Arab objections, it had become accepted that it has every right to exist within those borders. Territory captured from Egypt, Syria, and Jordan, including all of the West Bank, together with East Jerusalem as well as the Gaza Strip however, had to be returned. Israel itself, also, initially denied it had any territorial ambitions and in fact passed a military order declaring the Geneva Conventions to be applicable there. Its own legal department issued memoranda to that effect, declaring their opinion that Israeli annexation of, or settlement of its civilians in the occupied territories would be illegal.

As the Arab world slowly absorbed the lessons of 1967 and began to accept the reality of Israel's existence, their language also reflected this new understanding. Their claims shifted from calling for the liberation of Palestine to calling for the return of territories occupied in 1967. UN Resolutions 242 and 338 were passed unanimously by the Security Council and became the basis for an international consensus regarding both the status of the occupied territories and the basis for peace between Israel and its "Arab Neighbors." The PLO was also pressured, and eventually accepted this formula. It was also enshrined in the Arab Peace Initiative presented first by Saudi Arabia, and later accepted by all Arab and Islamic countries. Numerous UN resolutions, including Security Council resolutions also affirmed this reality. To try to change it would be a very difficult task indeed.

Meanwhile, the Israelis undermined this possibility by their actions on the ground. They tried to challenge its applicability to all the occupied territories and raised questions as to whether Palestinians or Jordan were to be beneficiaries of the return of the territories. At the same time, they continued to pay lip service to it as the official position of the Israeli government, as far as the rest of the world was concerned. For this reason alone, the near consensus of international law persisted, and currently presents one of the greatest challenges to anyone wishing to present an alternative to two-state solution.

Second: The Logic and Convenience of the Two-State Solution
For anyone considering the claims of both Zionists and Palestinian Nationalists, the two-state solution presents a comfortable, and convenient compromise, as did the initial Partition Resolution of 1947. It appears to be a reasonable compromise that reflects the realities on the ground. The outrages of the Holocaust and the desperate need of a Jewish population for a safe haven, which led to the creation and acceptance of the state of Israel, as well as the needs of the Palestinians for a state of their own both seem to be met by the two-state solution. It was not necessary to take sides or even to weigh the relative justice of each cause

or to delve into the nature of the state. The two-state solution seemed to satisfy both sides and avoided the need to confront or challenge either of them.

Third: Preserving Ideologies
The language of two-state solution leaves the battling ideologies intact, and only requires a geographic division and spatial limitation on the exercise of each ideology. Chauvinism, racism, discrimination and inherent problems are all swept under the rug. No real critique of either Zionism or Palestinian Nationalism is required, if we accept the language of the two-state solution.

Fourth: Enabling the Status Quo
The two-state solution provides a perfect alibi for the status quo. For fifty-three years now, Israel has been acting as a true sovereign in the occupied territories, without needing to grant its residents equal status or citizenship. It engages in a number of strategies to maintain the status quo without acknowledging the need to arrive at a solution. It squabbles over the specific requirements of international law and puts increasingly impossible demands on Palestinian leaders. Sometimes it pretends to be awaiting sufficient political will, international pressure, the rise of an "adequate partner" or the next elections to arrive at the proposed solution (two-state solution) while effectively undermining any possibility of its arrival. As long as the language of two-state solution persists, the status quo can continue indefinitely.

A friend of mine once told his Israeli and Zionist friends "Congratulations! You won. There will never be a Palestinian State. NOW WHAT?" The question was extremely uncomfortable and remained unanswered. Abandonment of the mirage of a two-state solution forces the issue and requires action. Waiting for a two-state solution, on the other hand, implies that the current situation is temporary, and exceptional, and removes the urgency of addressing it in any serious or radical way.

Fifth: Projecting an Image of Democratic Conflict
The opposition of the right-wing in Israel provides an opportunity to continue the charade and colonization of the West Bank while pretending that Israelis are divided between the Left which favors concessions to Palestinians, and the Right which opposes them. Outward attributes of statehood, like a flag, a passport or acceptance into international organizations, becomes a battlefield between these two factions. Meanwhile, granting true sovereignty for Palestinians is never seriously contemplated. The Right accuses Israeli governments of "giving them guns" while all Israeli governments expect them to use these guns only against their own people. Tidbits of authority are carefully doled out as favors or concessions, while true power remains in Israel's hands.

Sixth: Fear of Alternatives
Perhaps the strongest reason for using two-state solution language is the fear of the alternative and the need to maintain a taboo against one-state discussions. This is felt particularly among the Israeli leftists and liberal Zionists. The minute the two-state solution language is abandoned, the only real alternative is the idea of one state. To many Israeli liberals, as well as supporters of Israel worldwide, one state, if it is at all to be sustainable, will require a democratic "one person-one vote" component, which spells—in their minds—the end of the Jewish state and of Zionism. Some openly say this, and refuse to dialogue with anyone supporting one state, even attacking such a person as anti-semitic, or accusing them of calling for the destruction of the state of Israel. Palestinians have consistently been told that to have any chance of peace, they need to abandon any thought of

one state, and to work (against all odds) for a two-state solution. In this paradigm, the "demographic demon" (see Chapter 12) makes it impossible to talk of one state.

These legitimate arguments make it difficult to abandon the two-state solution and explain why the language of two-state solution persists and dominates the conversation, even among those who acknowledge that it has no chance of ever becoming a reality.

8: Minimum Requirements

Once we acknowledge that the two-state solution is no longer tenable and start seeking new solutions, it becomes necessary to consider what the minimum requirements are for each party. It is clear that neither Jewish Zionism, which requires an Israel as Jewish as France is French, nor Palestinian Nationalism, which insists that *Falastine Arabiyyeh* (Palestine is Arab), can get everything it wants. Yet it is worthwhile to consider the elemental, non-negotiable, minimum requirements of each side.

It is also important that these "requirements" take into account that the proposed solution must also accommodate the Other, and that each demand carries within it the possibility that the other side may legitimately respond with a parallel demand. The exercise is therefore also an invitation to consider how such demands can be met within a new reality that is open to another community of roughly equal numbers and legitimate demands of their own, rather than in the spirit of triumphal exclusivity. Those purists who insist on ignoring or denying the other party's legitimacy need not participate in this exercise. They will simply doom themselves and their people to eternal enmity and strife in a situation where neither party can be fully successful.

In this chapter, I will try to list these requirements, but acknowledge that I have made no scientifically accurate poll to determine the answers to this question, but instead am relying on individual observations and analysis of both communities.

Minimum Requirements for Jewish Israelis
As I see it, these are the minimum requirements for Jewish Israelis and Zionists generally:

A Home with a Law of Return. The whole purpose of creating the Zionist movement and the state of Israel was the perceived need to create a country that can act as a safe haven where any Jew, anywhere and at any time, can feel free to go and live there, as of right in a state of his/her own. No questions asked. Israel currently has such an ironclad law, which it considers to be a Basic Law of constitutional stature. It also has a publicly supported network of institutions supporting this right. They include a government ministry charged with absorbing, assimilating, providing housing and jobs, as well as language training for such new immigrants so that they can feel fully at home. This seems to be one irreducible requirement for Zionists and Israeli Jews.

Security. Given the experience of the Holocaust as well as millennia of antisemitic behavior in Christian Europe, including periodic pogroms and the Inquisition, security is an overriding consideration. Furthermore, the enmity and hostility involved in fighting the Palestinians and other Arabs since the creation of the State of Israel makes security considerations vital priorities that must be addressed in any new arrangement. They need to know that any new arrangement will provide lasting security, and is not just an interim ceasefire, but a real end to the conflict. I will be addressing these security considerations elsewhere, but here I am acknowledging that this is a heartfelt basic need and requirement for Jewish Israelis and Zionists generally.

A Jewish Rhythm to Public Life. Even secular Jews who resent restrictions imposed by the ultra-Orthodox, nonetheless have expressed a desire to live in a country where Saturday is the official Shabbat, life comes to a standstill on Yom Kippur, and where religious holidays are recognized and respected. They want a place where their tribal identity is recognized and where they can experience and develop Jewish communal life. To them, Zionism means a Jewish state, and a Jewish state reflects in some fashion a Jewish calendar, Jewish culture and a Jewish rhythm to public life.

Hebrew Language. In addition to culture, tribe, and rhythm of life, the Hebrew language is of vital importance. This has taken on much more importance than a hundred years ago when Hebrew was more of a liturgical language, and very few spoke it as a first language.

Right to Live anywhere in Israel/Palestine. Many Israelis have publicly expressed willingness, within the framework of a genuine peace along the lines of a two-state solution, to abandon some or all of the Jewish settlements in areas occupied in 1967. At the same time, the reality on the ground, with over 700,000 settlers living in those areas, as well as the historic and religious connection to such places as Hebron and Jerusalem indicate that no major displacement of settlers can take place. An unspoken requirement therefore is to permit Jews to have the same right to live in all parts of *Eretz Yisrael* as Palestinian Arabs.

Democracy. Israeli Jews will insist on the major elements of a liberal democracy. This includes the usual individual and collective freedoms: speech, religion, peaceful assembly, a free press, an independent judiciary, *representativ*e government, free elections, accountability of public officials, rule of law and the like. (Incidentally, I know of no Palestinian who would object to such principles, or who would not aspire to them as well).

Minimum Requirements for Palestinians
For their part, Palestinians forced to abandon the two-state solution compromise and to come to terms with Zionists, including

settlers, would insist that any future state manifest the following requirements:

Political and Legal Equality. As the weaker party, who have suffered much at the hands of Israel, both in Israel itself (pre-1967 borders) and in the occupied territories, the most pressing demand would be for iron-clad constitutionally protected equality. This equality should come with an effective mechanism to ensure its application in all areas of public life and resources. Particularly as Israeli Jews initially retain a majority and may demand certain guarantees and assurances in the area of security (for example), Palestinians would insist that the principle of equality be recognized as central. As the demographic balance may shift in the future, Jews may also find that they need the same ironclad assurances of equality if they should lose their numerical majority. They need to know that any concessions made to them will be protected from the whims or caprice of a future Arab majority.

Palestinians can initially agree to the current economic inequality, but over time, this is almost certain to change. The current economic disparity is augmented by the historical seizure of so many Palestinian resources such as water, arable land, and the sea. Reparations must eventually be considered as a way of addressing the current gross inequalities.

Right of Return for Refugees. While the majority of refugees are unlikely to move back to Israel/Palestine, all of them would insist on their right to return if they choose to do so. Just as American and European Jews may not be eager to give up their current lives in the West, but nonetheless insist on their Right of Return, so is it with Palestinians. It is inconceivable that Jews would insist on their "Right to Return" after two thousand years of exile, while

Palestinians are denied the same right to return to a homeland they lost within the living memory of most of them.

Right to Freely Move and Live in all Parts of Israel/Palestine. This would include the removal of all restrictions on rights of access to Jerusalem, the end of the siege of Gaza, the removal of the Wall, checkpoints, the military government, and the permit system currently governing their lives, as well as the freedom to travel.

Democracy. Palestinian aspirations for a genuinely democratic government are no less intense than that of the Jewish Israelis. Palestinians have a vibrant civil society and have learned a lot (positively and negatively) from interaction with Israelis, as well as from living under dictatorial Arab governments. Any claim that Palestinians are "not ready" for democracy or would accept and be satisfied with the repressive behavior of either the PA or Hamas is totally false.

Cultural Identity. The state has to acknowledge and respect Palestinian Arab identity, culture, language, and religious feelings. Many have argued that a Palestinian state with its flag and passport and symbols of sovereignty is an essential part of Palestinian nationalism. I would argue that while Palestinian identity is clearly important and recognition as a people with a distinct identity is essential, statehood as such is not. The brief and unimpressive experience with the Palestinian National Authority, without in any way reducing Palestinian Arab Nationalism, has dampened the desire for nominal statehood as such. Palestinians want the benefits that come from sovereign independence and self-determination. If they can be achieved without statehood, Palestinians are willing to consider it. The need is for self-determination, freedom and recognition of identity. If a "state" fails to provide that, then a "state" is neither required nor will be sufficient. If these can be achieved in a binational context, or in a state that is not exclusively Arab or Palestinian, I believe most of us would be quite satisfied.

Arabic Language. Arabic would be recognized equally with Hebrew as a national language.

֍

Can these minimum requirements of both communities be met within a single unitary state? I believe they can, and this is the entire premise of this book. The specific vision I will propose may not be the right one, and there may be other formulations offered by others, but any proposal should attempt to meet all the above needs if it is to have any chance of acceptance, much less stability and survival.

9: The Vision

"If you want it, it is not a legend."
Theodor Herzl

So then, what is the alternative, once we give up on the two-state solution?

I personally have a vision for a new state that addresses the needs both of Israeli Jews and Palestinian Arabs. I believe this proposal addresses the needs of both communities, though achieving it may be an entirely different matter.

Ideology
The vision is for a new entity, a hybrid state, a unique entity in all of the land of historic Palestine/*Eretz Yisrael*. This entity would embrace and validate the essential elements of both Zionism and Palestinian Nationalism, while rejecting those elements in each movement which degrade or deny the Other. It is a vision for a vibrant democracy for all its citizens, where citizens can both be proud of their unique individual and collective identities, but where they are prohibited from forcing such identities on others.

Religion
The vision will respect and recognize all three monotheistic religions and provide free access to people of all religions to their holy places in the Land. It will also respect any among its citizens who do not choose to believe in any religion, or who do not wish to be constrained by the religious group they grew up with. Friday and Saturday will be official holidays, but Christians will be allowed by law to take half a day off on Sunday for worship if they choose. A national calendar acknowledging the major religious

holidays of all three religions will be published and respected. It will include 10 official holidays where all government offices are closed, with 4 additional days of "selective holidays" to be taken at the discretion of each employee covering additional days when his/her important holidays are not on the official calendar.

Religious Courts
The new state will allow those who wish, as individuals or collective groups, to practice and order their lives in accordance with their religion. But it will also provide a secular system for personal status matters (marriage, divorce, inheritance) to those who do not wish to be bound by the religious strictures of their particular group. It will NOT allow any group to impose its will on the others, or on unwilling members of its own group in those vital matters. That means that a dual system of courts will handle personal status matters: religious and secular. The first shall be voluntary, and the second obligatory, and available to all. A person desiring a halachic, ecclesiastical or sharii' wedding is free to obtain one, and the marriage will be recognized by the state and the secular courts automatically. A person who does not desire to continue to be religiously bound, may seek a secular divorce (or write his or her own will) which will be recognized by the secular authorities even if their religious authorities do not consider it valid. In their eyes, for example, a lady obtaining a secular divorce would be considered still married and cannot remarry in a religious ceremony of her faith community. But in the eyes of the secular courts she is legitimately divorced and can remarry and proceed with her life.

A similar situation prevails in the US today and is perfectly acceptable. A Catholic can obtain a secular divorce, and will be free to remarry, but will not be able to obtain a Catholic church wedding as the church does not recognize his or her secular divorce. This will be a vast improvement over the current situation where "unrecognized" communities such as Conservative and Reform Jews, Baha'is, Christian Evangelicals with their many denominations and Jehovah Witnesses cannot perform marriages or order their personal affairs properly. It will also help an Orthodox Jewish woman to obtain a divorce if her recalcitrant husband refuses to grant her a *get* (religious divorce).

Elections and Governance
As a democracy, the new entity will be governed by a legislative council in the form of a Parliament, freely elected by universal adult suffrage. This will be bound by an iron-clad constitution that is deliberately crafted to ensure majority rule, but which will safeguard basic freedoms of the individual, as well as minorities from the caprice of the majority. It is hoped that over time, more and more individuals will vote and elect representatives who reflect their views on diverse issues, and not merely vote on the basis of their ethnic or religious identity. If I run for elections, for example, I would hope that many Jews would vote for me, based on my record of human rights advocacy and my politics of moderation and reconciliation. I also know that I would rather vote for a Jewish candidate who cares about the environment and about peace and tolerance and other issues that reflect my own values, than for a bigoted Palestinian. A religious Moslem may feel a particular Jewish religious candidate better reflects her views on pivotal issues than a secular Palestinian, and so forth...

Basic Rights
The Constitution will guarantee a number of basic rights to all citizens, including the standard human rights to freedom of movement, speech, association and freedom of religion, and the like.

It will also emphasize in particular a number of principles uniquely important in our context: For example, freedom to live in any part of the country and to leave the country and to return to it, will be safeguarded in the Constitution. The Right of Return for anyone of Jewish or Palestinian ancestry will be guaranteed, and not subject to parliamentary restriction by whoever is in the majority. A Constitutional Court composed of five judges, at least two of whom shall be Jewish and two Arab, shall deal with constitutional matters and must reach all decisions by a 4/5th majority.

Equality before the Law
In addition, the Constitution will provide for guarantees protecting full equality, and a prohibition on all forms of discrimination in the public sphere. There will be an exception for those provisions in the Constitution deliberately inserted to reassure groups against the caprice of a current or future majority. The provisions in the Constitution shall have precedence over all other legislation and can only be varied by super majorities. The constitutional court will hear challenges to any legislation, regulation or practice which contravenes its provisions. While no law can change what is in the hearts of people, and the struggle for equality and against racism and prejudice will continue, the law should be clearly on the side of equality. In the public sphere, it is possible to outlaw discrimination in employment, resource allocation, governmental services, land and water usage, and the like. Discretionary power for any public official shall be severely restricted where discrimination or bias is involved.

Military
For reasons discussed before, relating both to millennia of anti-semitic persecution culminating in the Holocaust, and decades of conflict with the Palestinians and neighboring Arab countries,

Jewish fears need to be addressed forthrightly. The Constitution will require that a Jewish person will always head the Ministry of Defense, the Army, the Navy, the Air force and the Atomic Energy Administration. Each such Minister shall have an Arab deputy. All other positions in the Armed forces shall be open to all citizens strictly on the basis of merit. Any individual not wishing to serve in the armed forces shall have the option of doing Civilian Service instead. The head of the Police Force, on the other hand, shall always be an Arab, with a Jewish deputy, as the Arabs have also had a traumatic history of discrimination and oppression by the Israeli Police.

Ministry of Cooperation and Coexistence
A designated Government Ministry will actively work to foster understanding between the communities by teaching the history and culture of each community to the other and by promoting joint projects. This Ministry shall also carry out deliberate attempts to ameliorate or overcome the results of previous discrimination. This will include efforts to integrate Arabs in spheres, institutions and industries (including the army) where they had been in the past prohibited from entering. Preventing communal strife must not be left to the goodwill of ordinary people but must be made a collective priority of the state and considerable resources must be applied to it. No less than ten percent of the defense budget should go to this ministry since security is indeed a vital concern, and the danger to the safety of individual Jews, in particular, comes primarily from internal threats fostered by decades of hatred and conflict.

Reparations and Compensation
During the history of the struggle, many Palestinians lost their homes and lands, and many Jews are living in such homes, or on

such lands. As Palestinian refugees return, this injustice should be addressed. To resettle Palestinian refugees, compensate for lands which had been expropriated from them, and which are currently fully utilized by the Other, the government shall work to resettle these refugees by providing either compensation or alternative housing or land—possibly from public lands. Such a plan would go a long way to address the sense of injustice, without displacing or endangering the living conditions of Jews who have settled into previously Arab-owned houses and lands and who have built their lives upon them. This would further reduce the anger, enmity and frustration and therefore contribute to security and safety as well as goodwill between the two communities. It must be acknowledged that absolute justice will never be achieved, but we can still address this major grievance and achieve relative justice and progress as we look to a common future.

Relations with World Jewry and the Arab World
The new state will continue to hold a special place for Jews worldwide, and to be important to all Jews who can look to it for cultural and religious focus, as well as a possible refuge in case of antisemitism and discrimination. It will also act as a bridge to the Arab and Moslem world for Jews. At the same time, the new state will act as a center of progressive life that can impact the Arab world. Palestinians can still be proud members of the Arab nation, while providing a progressive model for tolerant and enlightened life in the modern world. If successful, this vision will point to a new way for the Arabs to interact with the West, while maintaining their identity, dignity, and culture.

A Vision of Mutual Enrichment
Most of this essay has tried to meet the needs of Zionists and Arab Nationalists while requiring minimal derogations and

compromises from their ideologies to accommodate the Other. I would like to point out that there may well be advantages to this model for each community, besides the peace and security that come from ending the conflict. I would like to think that for a true Palestinian nationalist, this proposal would offer a view of Arab nationalism that is richer, more nuanced, and far more attractive than a straightforward Palestinian Arab State would provide. An Arab state that is open to the world and to other cultures and peoples revives and recalls the glorious days when the Arab and Moslem state was open to other idea and was a center for learning and sharing other cultures and languages.

For Zionists, also, I would like to think that a vision of Jewish life that is also enriched and enhanced by fully accepting and embracing Palestinians Arabs would be a more vibrant and authentic life which is genuinely a "light unto the nations." It would cease to be a ghetto and a foreign isolated Western implant in the heart of a hostile Middle East. Can we dream that Jewish life and Palestinian life can be made more, rather than less, by shedding exclusivity and embracing the Other in a unique new hybrid form of government that asserts the humanity and goodness of others, instead of assuming that the others are enemies to be feared, shunned and hated?

For both communities, classic theories hold that a nation-state dominated or exclusively run for and in the interest exclusively of their particular community is the "gold standard" to be sought and fought for. That thinking has not worked well for either community. Is it not time to reconsider that core tenet and instead seek an ideology that pursues identity—but not on an exclusive basis: an identity that is enriched by, and relishes interaction with the Other, rather than seeks to deny and delegitimize it? Perhaps in shedding exclusivity, we would not lose, but gain a richer identity and a better life for our people as well as the Other. Xenophobia can be a powerful force for enhancing group identity, but at some point, as here, it becomes toxic and destructive, and shedding it may well be the preferred option, for each community.

10: Constitutional Guarantees

A constitution is the seminal founding document for any society that is run by democratic principles and the Rule of Law.

Inherent in the very word, constitution, is the idea that this document lays the groundwork for the running of society, which is expected to last for centuries. It creates the framework for resolving major issues in society. It is not subject to altering moods of the population, or the different governments, and legislatures, or the whims of the electorate.

For this reason, there needs to be broad acceptance of a constitution by all significant stakeholders in society, and it must stand above ordinary laws and regulations. It should be interpreted by independent courts, including a Constitutional Court. It can only be altered, or amended through an elaborate process, that includes perhaps a much higher supermajority of legislators, and a plebiscite or other form of ensuring that the amendments partake of the same solemnity and long-lasting nature as the constitution itself.

In the current situation in Israel/Palestine, a constitution is a necessary element in any long-term resolution of the conflict. It should guarantee the deepest elements agreed upon as basic for both communities, as well as assurances that such interests will continue to be guarded and respected by all future governments. Its provisions should hold, regardless of the shifting political views and future events and changes, including the potential changes in demographic composition. Such change may result from birth rates, exercise of Right of Return, immigration and emigration from the State, as well as regional changes. It must also guarantee each individual, as well as each community, against the whims of the majority both now and in the future.

In Chapter Eight, I outlined what I considered to be a number of essential features and interests that each party would insist upon in any long-term solution. These should be enshrined in the constitution, not just as aspirational guiding principles but compulsory binding requirements that trump and overrule any future legislation that is incompatible with them. The actual constitution will end up being the subject of serious negotiations between the parties, and every article in it carefully worded and negotiated, but I think it should contain specific reference to the following elements and guarantees:

Right of Return for Jews as well as Palestinians
The constitution will recognize and guarantee the right of return for both communities. Other provisions in the constitution will ensure that the exercise of that right by either community will not negate the rights of the other community regardless of the numerical shift it may cause.

Recognition of the Historic and Cultural Connection of both Jews and Arabs to the Land
Both the Israeli Declaration of Independence and the current Palestinian Constitution contain beautiful language relating to the connection between the People and the Land. Similar language can be drafted that also asserts such connection for each group without denying the other. This is a major departure from both Palestinian Nationalism, and Zionism, each of which negated or neglected and did not recognize any national rights for the other group. The Constitution will also enshrine respect for both Arabic and Hebrew languages.

Religious Freedom
The Constitution would provide an appreciation of the three monotheistic religions and a clear statement of religious freedom for both religious communities and for individuals whose religious identity does not fit within the recognized groups. This includes, for Jews the rights of Reform, Conservative, Orthodox, and secular Jews. For Christians, this includes the rights of all denominations, not just the currently recognized list of churches. For Shiites, Baha'is, Druze, and secular people, the Constitution not only guarantees freedom of religion for all, but also freedom from religion for those with no religious faith.

A secular system of civil laws in personal status matters will be instituted side by side with religious courts for those who choose to follow them. For example, non-Orthodox Jews will not be forced to follow Orthodox rabbinical courts in their personal status matters and likewise for Christians, whose churches are not recognized or who may choose not to follow their particular denomination's strictures regarding divorce, and so for Moslems, who choose to write their own wills, rather than be governed by Sharia rules for distribution of their estates. The right formula can be found that recognizes and respects all religions and also allows secular laws to govern those who do not choose to follow the religious strictures of their ethnic/religious communities or faith.

In some secular countries, like France, there is an animosity towards religion in public life. In the United States, by contrast, there is a separation of Church and State that preserves religious freedom while giving superiority to secular laws.

Guarantee of Equality
Equality would be guaranteed for all citizens in all areas of public life, except for the specific provisions agreed upon in the Constitution itself, for example in the area of security.

11: Objections and Challenges

This has been an intellectual exercise in determining if it is possible to map out a vision of a solution that addresses the most basic needs of both communities. It requires a radical rethinking of the ideologies governing both sides. As such, it is clear there will be those on both sides, not to mention numerous actors from outside the area, who will oppose this vision and work to prevent it from gaining any legitimacy or acceptance. I am not concerned here with those who insist on negating the Other, and who will not be satisfied with any solution that does not allow them to dominate or negate the other group. I am more concerned with those genuinely seeking peace and reconciliation who still find this vision objectionable.

Apart from the genuine obstacles that would prevent ANY peaceful resolution of this conflict, which I will address elsewhere, there are still serious objections even on a theoretical level, which I will attempt to list and address here:

There is Absence of a Model
It is argued that no historical or current model exists where two or more diverse ethnic and religious communities have successfully created a peaceful and stable form of coexistence. Sooner, or later, it is argued, conflict arises leading to civil war, secession, or oppression by one group of the other.

The truth, however, is that there are several models where diverse communities have existed in peaceful cooperation. I do not simply refer to situations like Lebanon, where a complex multi-ethnic constitution tried to balance the different groups, with difficulty. I also do not refer to the failed Yugoslav tri-cameral system where only a strong General Tito could keep Serbs, Muslims, and Croats at peace, until he died and the country split into warring entities. Instead, I refer to pluralistic countries like Canada, Belgium, Northern Ireland, and the current United States, where, with faltering steps, a multi-ethnic society was established. Despite continuing low-level tensions, racism and discrimination by the majority, minorities have found legal protection and spaces to survive, and thrive and feel identity as stakeholders in the national enterprise.

But even if no successful model exists, the very uniqueness of the situation in the Holy Land, calls for a unique response and a new vision, a vision which would not only address the conflicting demands but also provide much, by way of example, to the surrounding countries and peoples. There is much in the history and tradition of both communities that can be called upon and given concrete form. The desire of Israeli Jews to provide a "light to the nations" and draw on their prophetic and ethical tradition, as well as their centuries of experience as persecuted minorities can be a source of inspiration and strength. Jewish Torah teachings about proper treatment of the stranger in their midst can also be tapped to support systems of equality and tolerance. The Arab tradition of hospitality to strangers and history of tolerance towards minorities is also rich and noteworthy. The experience of the Palestinians with diaspora, struggle, and interaction with multiple societies in the Arab region and throughout the world has taught them much as well. By drawing on these strands in history and culture, rather than tribalism, and the uglier exclusivities and rejection of the Other, the new entity will have much to teach the surrounding countries. All of the neighboring countries face simmering problems of dealing with their own minorities (Kurds, Shiites, Yazidis, Berbers, Assyrians, Druze and Maronites) all of whom seek to assert their identities and are tempted to rebel and seek an autonomous if not independent national existence. They also struggle with issues of modernism, secularism and seeking to separate religion from the state. If both Palestinian Arabs and Zionist Jews can manage to forge a new reality that satisfies their identities without negating the other, then other peoples in the Middle East can hope to find satisfaction within their own countries as well.

It is a Dangerous Neighborhood
This is a variant of the first objection which points out that the people in this part of the world harbor ancient animosities and are not prone to accept a "civilized" solution. It is argued that they have been acculturated into trusting only the language of force and are not easily persuaded to accept liberal and enlightened solutions that may work in a "western" or modern context.

This argument smacks of racism as well as ignorance. The history and traditions of Arabs, Moslems, and Jews, while containing some ugly episodes, also have much that supports tolerance and coexistence. In fact, the historical record shows long periods of peaceful coexistence which far exceed the few instances and periods of intolerance. It is perhaps human nature to focus on the ugly instances of repression, persecution, and intolerance rather than the longer periods of tolerance and fruitful coexistence.

There is Over-Reliance on Legal Mechanisms
It may be argued that this vision places too much emphasis on a constitution and legal structures which are only pieces of paper, after all. It is true that laws and documents alone cannot guarantee a happy outcome and that violent forces often overthrow established laws and ignore or change constitutions to meet their current desires. However, a carefully drafted arrangement,

which is approved by large segments of the population of both sides and is enshrined in a constitution, has a good chance of survival. It becomes a focal starting point, gains stature, obtains international legitimacy, and becomes sustainable as it gets interpreted and implemented by an independent and respected judiciary.

The reason constitutions and laws are often ineffective in many Middle Eastern countries is that they are not viewed as legitimate sources of authority. They are commonly ignored by the executive branch, which also controls and dictates to the judiciary. The vision we are proposing contemplates a democratic society governed by the Rule of Law. It requires an independent judiciary, buttressed by a free press and a professional civil service that follows judicial decisions, and where the executive is not above the law. It also requires a vibrant civil society which actively monitors the behavior of the government and its agencies and has the ability to petition for legal redress.

Even in the most stable and robust of democracies, a vigilant citizenry is required to constantly ensure that society lives up to its stated ideals. Such ideals need to be clearly stated and written into a formal constitution, which does not leave serious issues unanswered. In the present situation in Israel, no constitution exists, and a plethora of Emergency Regulations grant wide discretion to the executive branch to destroy property, imprison people without charges or trial, exercise collective punishment, and confiscate property. This would be as unacceptable as the model of Arab countries with beautifully worded constitutions which are merely aspirational and are routinely ignored by the rulers and unenforceable in courts. Fortunately, both Palestinians and Israelis have developed robust civil societies and have populations that aspire for a far more democratic structure than currently exists.

Why Should the Stronger Party Accept this Solution?
It is argued that the Zionist movement has succeeded in capturing all of historic Palestine and controls all the levers of power. It enjoys total domination in all sectors with overwhelming superiority, and there is little challenge to this superiority from the Palestinians, the Arab world, or the international community. Furthermore, under the Trump administration, it had the chance to further consolidate its power and even openly annex large portions of the occupied territories, so why should it risk or abandon all its hard-won victories and privileges?

The answer is that despite all its success, the current situation is neither stable nor sustainable in the long term. The current situation is that only one state, Israel, exists between the Jordan River and the Mediterranean Sea. In that state, Jews have rights and privileges, which can only be sustained by brute physical force and at the expense of the Palestinian Arab population. In effect, it constitutes apartheid and oppression which history tells us cannot forever be sustained and has the direct effect of being cruel. The ability of Israel to claim to be a democracy in an increasingly interrelated world order is wearing thin.

A dominant group does not give up its privileges easily or voluntarily but must feel internal or external pressure (whether military, economic, or otherwise) before it adjusts its behavior. The power imbalance between Palestinians and Israeli Jews must be addressed before ANY solution can be pursued. This was also true for the two-state solution, and for any other proposed solution. Ultimately both sides must be coerced or convinced that peace, rather than vanquishing the Other, is the only long-term solution. Until Israelis are convinced that the status quo is not sustainable, they have no incentive to change it. In a way, it is precisely the military success of the Zionist movement that now stands in the way of fulfilling the deepest desires for peace, legitimacy, acceptance, and ultimate survival of their project.

The Depth of Enmity Makes any Solution Unlikely
One of the greatest obstacles to any peace agreement is the prevailing despair that many people feel. We are told that the enmity and hatred between the two groups is too deep and profound to permit for any peace between them, and therefore the best we can hope for is for temporary truces and accommodations. One Israeli right-winger once told me that if Arabs had done to him what Israel has done to them he would never forgive them, and would only bide his time until he got his revenge. This was his justification for refusing to compromise or make any accommodation. He viewed peace as impossible and therefore wanted to obtain maximum advantage and maintain maximum vigilance.

My response is that while I recognize the depth of hostility and mistrust between the parties, yet history is full of instances of mortal enemies who killed millions of each other, and yet who eventually became friends and allies. Germans and French fought pitched battles and destroyed whole cities for each other within living memory, yet today they are allies and friends. There is no reason to think that the same cannot be true for Palestinians and Israeli Jews once a just solution is reached that addresses their deepest needs.

A Minority Cannot Survive or Thrive in Israel/Palestine
The driving force behind the Zionist idea was that Jews can never be safe except in a state of their own, where they are the masters

and dominant power, and where they can guard and protect their bastion against all outside enemies. This fear was fed by the failure of even progressive countries to defend and protect their Jewish minorities and by the persistent antisemitism that flared again and again with fatal consequences for Jewish communities.

Palestinians, too, have not been welcomed with open arms by their Arab brethren, and for their part, too, there is the feeling that they can never feel safe nor aspire to their national potential except in a Palestinian State of their own, in their own land, where they are the majority, and as lords and masters, can determine their own fate.

It is true that minorities are often discriminated against, denied full citizenship rights, denied equal access to education, work, health care, are scapegoated and persecuted for society's problems, and in worst cases subject to mass expulsion and murder. We cannot understate what minorities may suffer.

Yet this is not a universal law, and there are many instances where minorities are not only tolerated and welcomed, but where they are considered essential elements in society. There are many examples in world history where minorities have thrived within different societies, and its members held positions of power and responsibility. This is also true for the Middle East. The modern world currently has some minorities who not only enjoy full rights and citizenship, but who also have prominence and leadership in major sectors of the societies in which they live. Palestinian immigrants in some Latin American countries enjoy great power, influence and wealth.

In the United States, Canada, and some other Western countries today, despite the persistent existence of antisemitism, Jewish citizens enjoy respect and influence. As an ethnic group they have economic and political influence far beyond their numbers. In the US today, though the Jewish community is only 3 percent of the population, on matters such as the Israeli/Palestinian conflict, aid to Israel, voting at the United Nations and international fora, their influence is so strong that most observers cannot envision a US policy in the Middle East that does not reflect their wishes.

12: False Democracy and the Demographic Demon

The Hazards of a False Understanding of Democracy

One of the reasons the idea of a two-state solution persists, and there is such great reluctance to consider other alternatives is because of a false notion of what democracy entails. This concept is prevalent in the Middle East and much of the rest of the world as well. Under this faulty concept, democracy is primarily about elections allowing a 51% majority of voters to determine all matters in a particular country. The democratically elected government can then proceed to ignore, crush, stigmatize, disenfranchise, demonize, or even criminalize the rest of the population.

A more accurate view of democracy recognizes that while a majority of voters in free and periodic open elections can choose representatives who will both legislate and govern, there are other factors that go into a true democracy. These include the rule of law, a free press, transparent and accountable government, an independent judiciary. They also include a careful system of checks and balances, as well as iron-clad constitutional guarantees that provide both the individual citizen and the minorities substantial freedoms and inviolable rights. Democracy needs to protect citizens and their interests from the caprice of volatile majorities and pernicious flare-ups of populist sentiments that may be exploited by demagogues.

Examples of this misunderstanding abound: America claimed to be bringing democracy to Iraq, and mandated an election there, which Nouri al-Maliki, a Shiite, won. He then proceeded to create a primarily Shiite government, ignoring the rights of the Sunnis, who had dominated Iraqi politics for generations, as well as the Kurds and other minorities. The result was discontent that caused a surprising alliance between the Sunnis and ISIS which took control of over a third of the country in a matter of weeks. This rendered the central government in Baghdad almost powerless, while the Kurds moved quickly to establish a virtually autonomous government in their own region in the North. The result was not a democracy at all.

A similar process took place in Egypt, after the fall of Hosni Mubarak in the Arab Spring. Hasty elections led to a victory by Mohammad Morsi of the Moslem Brotherhood, the only organized force at the time. The Brotherhood then proceeded to set the stage for a Moslem state in Egypt, reportedly claiming that since they had "democratically" come into power, they would ensure that Egypt would continue under Moslem Brotherhood rule for 500 years. The rest of the population rebelled, and before a single year was over the military took power with "popular support," and in the name of the "majority of the people" overthrew the Morsi regime and began to entrench themselves. The new president, Abdel Fattah Saeed Hussein Khalil el-Sisi, then proceeded to arrest and suppress freedoms of all parties, not just the Moslem Brotherhood, who turned to an underground movement and an insurrection. Neither Morsi nor el-Sisi offered the true democracy which the Egyptian people wanted and deserved.

In Palestine, Fatah and Hamas seem to follow the same logic. Upon winning elections, first one then the other tried to take control of all organs of government and to rule with little or no appreciation for the other party, or for the majority of Palestinians who were not affiliated with either of the two parties. When Fatah lost the elections, Hamas tried to push them out of power.

When they refused, it resorted to an armed takeover in Gaza, leaving both areas—the West Bank and Gaza—to be ruled undemocratically by each of the two factions respectively. Thirteen years have passed since the last elections, and each party is entrenched in its respective area, with little concern for democracy or for the Palestinian people.

In the conflict between Palestinian nationalists and Zionist Jews, the issue is even more sharply focused. The general feeling is that every individual should, and can be counted upon, to vote and exercise power in a uniform tribal fashion in support of his/her ethnic group and against the other group. In this zero-sum thinking, demography becomes the seminal factor, and the demographic demon becomes an existential threat to the very essence of each group. By the magic of democracy, each group believes that all it needs is to achieve numerical dominance over the other. If the demographic balance changes, the entire power relationship would be reversed, and the dominant oppressor of today, becomes an oppressed and marginalized minority. The fear that a minority is not only left without rights but can be literally obliterated and ethnically cleansed by the majority group lurks in the consciousness and subconscious of many groups in the area. The fate of Yezidis and Christians in Iraq, of Kurds, and of other groups elsewhere only reinforces this fear. Many Zionists state that in light of their historical experience, Jews can ill-afford ever to be in a minority.

Caught in the throes of this type of thinking, one is tempted to throw out the concept of democracy altogether and insist on domination by sheer brute force and power, regardless of numbers. The alternative is to see the conflict between the two groups as purely a demographic conflict. Every additional immigrant strengthens one party, and every additional child born, revives the hopes of the other party to eventually turn the tables and become the dominant oppressor.

It is my contention that this view of demography does not at all reflect genuine democracy, but it also is not accurate, in terms of the real world.

Demography does not Determine Power in a Truly Democratic Society
While it is true that democracies are built around elections and votes, and that numbers are significant in determining outcomes of elections, yet demographics alone do not determine election outcomes, and elections alone do not determine all issues of power in a democratic society. Ethnic groups do not always vote as a block, for one of their own. Throughout the Western world, substantial minorities often suffer from underrepresentation, and routinely complain that significant sectors of society, the economy and the power structures are not open to them. In the alternative, they are only represented there by a token few who do not always reflect the interests of their minority community. Other minorities, however, are represented far beyond their numbers in the governing structures of the country, and in the centers of effective power within it. At the same time, immigrants find that it takes a couple of generations of integration before they fully participate in political life and become sufficiently accepted into the halls of power. By contrast, other minority groups wield influence totally beyond their numbers.

A perfect example of this phenomenon is the United States. American Jews have obtained significant influence in the United States through education, wealth, internal solidarity and cohesion, focused concentration in certain significant sectors of life, civil institutions, and organized involvement in public life. On the other hand, American Moslems, of a roughly equal number demographically, are practically non-existent in the corridors of power and influence. It is in the very nature of democratic life to guarantee minorities the right to organize peacefully, and to improve their lot, both as a group and as individuals. However, it does not automatically distribute power proportionately along ethnic or religious lines. Systemic discrimination and obstacles to advancement are attacked as undemocratic, and citizens of all shades participate in campaigns and actions to eliminate such discrimination and bias. The goal is to allow all citizens to participate freely and advance naturally within society, regardless of the wishes or prejudices of the numerical majorities.

The principle of "one-person-one-vote" is at the heart of democracy, but it only provides for equal opportunity, while a myriad of other factors go into determining the true outcome and power-sharing. When structural and legal discrimination prevents people from advancing, as was the case in apartheid South Africa, the struggle was correctly conducted for removing the offending laws and instituting one-man-one-vote. But when that battle was won, and Nelson Mandela was elected President of South Africa, that did not give him and the ANC dictatorial control over the country. The Whites, (now a distinct numerical voting minority) were not disenfranchised, repressed, oppressed or thrown out of the country. In many ways, they continued to dominate certain sectors of the country and its economy, and the ANC found that it had many other challenges to meet as the new majority government of South Africa. One of the most interesting results of the end of Apartheid was that it did not lead to the demise of the White population, which continued to thrive. It also did not automatically end inequality within the country simply by removing the official legal discrimination that had previously been its basis.

True Democracy Provides Protections and Guarantees to Individuals and Minorities

Democracy provides for majority rule, but a genuine democracy does not permit legal discrimination against minorities, and it provides legal mechanisms for such minorities to demand their rights and oppose organized discrimination and bias in the public sphere. Whether by constitutional provisions or by long-standing traditions, a true democracy ensures that minorities are integrated into the body politic, and that their distinctive language, culture, religion, and customs can be exercised in freedom and dignity. Where such guarantees do not exist, the minority will feel alienated and oppressed, and the results inevitably are either civil war, or calls for secession and breakup. This happens when such minorities strive to fulfill their identities and achieve self-determination outside the common structures and in opposition to the majorities they feel are oppressing them.

Where different groups coexist in one country, genuine democracy provides for a multi-ethnic and pluralistic society. In such a society, individuals and substantial minorities can fully belong to the country while maintaining a feeling of belonging and identification with their own group which is respected by society as a whole. Whether that identity is ethnic, religious, linguistic, or regional, the majority do well to respect and acknowledge it, rather than dominate, marginalize or obliterate it. Only then, can the majority count on the loyalty of the minorities, while the minority feels a full sense of citizenship and belonging. Democratic societies that have historically disenfranchised and marginalized substantial groups, inevitably face a determined effort to bring such groups into the mainstream.

In the Israeli/Palestinian context, it is clear that no peaceful co-existence can be achieved until the demographic demon is put to rest. The fulfillment of each community must not be jeopardized by the obsession with achieving numerical majority or the dream that such majority status will allow them to negate or obliterate the rights of the other group. Once that truth sinks in, the Right of Return (for Jews and for Palestinian Arabs) will no longer be a frightening taboo, and a non-negotiable item. Declining or rising birth rates will be noted as sociological factors, rather than harbingers of cataclysmic political change. Each group will be free to pursue its destiny without fear of being blocked by a majority on the other side. Most importantly, the decision of every individual or family to live in the Land or to live abroad will be undertaken as an individual family or personal decision based on a myriad of economic, social, educational and family requirements. It will cease to be viewed primarily as a political decision in support of a presumed national agenda in favor of its group or the enemy group. The "battle of the womb" will also be put to rest, and a more normal life can proceed.

That certainly is not the case now. It will only become true when the false view of democracy is repudiated, and when constitutional and other guarantees are implemented that will effectively shield the minority (whether Arab or Jewish) from the caprice of a numerical majority. The vision is for a genuine democracy where both groups thrive, and not for an unstable system where elections are held, if at all, simply to validate and legitimize the power of one side to negate and dominate the other.

13: Unique Features

There are many countries where different ethnic, religious, and racial communities live together in the same nation-state. Such countries often face major disruptions, civil wars, calls for secession, and suppression and injustice. This occurs when the dominant group (not always the numerical majority) either seeks to maintain domination and control, negates and delegitimizes the others, or seeks unjust formulas for social peace and coexistence. Most of the history and examples are not very encouraging as tribal allegiances seem stronger than universal values and empathy with others.

In the Palestine/Israel context, however, there are several elements that make the problem different from most other situations, and solutions tried elsewhere may not necessarily work (or fail) in our context.

The new state that we can seek to visualize once we give up on the two-state solution will need to deal with each of these three elements:

First: The Nature of the Relationship between Palestine and the Arab World
Palestine lies geographically at the heart of the Arab world, being the bridge between the Levant countries and the Northern African countries. Not only is this position geographically in the heart of the Arab world, but since the rise of the Arab nationalist movement and anti-colonial movements, the question of Palestine was at the heart of the Arab world. It is not an accident that George Antonius, who wrote *The Arab Awakening*, and was viewed as the father of modern Arab Nationalism grew up in

Jerusalem. It has often been said that Palestine will either be the cement which binds the Arab World together or the dynamite that will blow it apart.

The role of Palestine and its place in the hearts and minds of the Arab peoples cannot be overestimated.

The dispersion of Palestinian refugees throughout the Arab world contributed to this phenomenon. Fully two-thirds of Palestinians today have sunk their roots, and largely become part of their "host countries" without forgetting their identity. Their contribution in building the Gulf States and Saudi Arabia, as well as the centrality of the Palestine question in the struggle between the Arab national movement and the Western world is well known and documented. Even before the time of Jamal Abdel Nasser, and into the time of the Moslem Brotherhood and the Islamic movements sweeping throughout the Arab world today, this continued to be the case. As the West supported the Zionist program in Israel, the plight of the Palestinian people and their heroic struggle was often seen as the forefront of the struggles of the Arab World for liberation and independence. In this respect, Palestine was always a surrogate, as well as pioneer for the entire Arab World. As Palestinians seek a new reality in combination with Jewish Israelis, we must be cognizant of this element.

Second: The Relationship between Jewish Israelis and the Worldwide Jewish Diaspora
The Zionist movement and the State of Israel was formulated as a response to worldwide antisemitism. It was promoted as a refuge and potential champion and rescuer for Jews worldwide. It also fully depended on support of all forms from this diaspora. Jews insist that they are full and loyal citizens of whatever

country they reside in, and correctly reject as antisemitic charges of dual loyalty.

At the same time, there is no question of the special relationship most Jews feel towards the state of Israel, and the security it gives them that it is available as a last resort if antisemitism ever again makes their survival in these countries untenable. The trauma of the Holocaust—when they suffered genocide and found no country to give them refuge—has been one of the most powerful drivers of Zionism and the state of Israel. It continues to haunt many Jews, even those living in security and power in Western countries. As Israel ceases to be an exclusively Jewish state (as it must, with the failure of the two-state solution), the role it plays for diaspora Jews would need to be acknowledged and addressed.

Third: Israel/Palestine is the Cradle of the Three Monotheistic Religions
The historical and religious significance of this location for adherents of all three religions throughout history has been both a blessing and a curse for the inhabitants of the Holy Land. This was particularly true when members of one of the three religions laid exclusive religious claims to the land in the name of God and sought to rid it of the "infidels" (namely the adherents of the other two religions). The Christian Crusades were perhaps the most outrageous form of this phenomena, although both Moslem and Jewish communities, when in power, have also exhibited clear inclinations in that direction. One reason that the conflict has persisted is that each side has had material, emotional and diplomatic support from actors outside the area who viewed the struggle as essential to them and to their faith.

These Three Elements Can Empower a Just Solution
We need to recognize the adherents of all three religions as serious stakeholders in this disputed Land. Their access for reasons of pilgrimage, as well as their support for their coreligionists in the Holy Land will have to be accommodated and acknowledged as part of any durable settlement.

The challenge is to use each of these three elements as a positive contributing factor in the interest of all the local population. This can be done by removing the "exclusive" component of these legitimate interests and using the clout of these outside elements as contributing to stability and prosperity rather than instability and intolerance. Such powerful outside forces can also guarantee the successful implementation of any agreed upon formula, (once achieved) and thereby reduce the need to assert local dominance and numerical demographic superiority. The existence, influence and power of such outside forces can both provide a valuable resource, as well as guarantees for ongoing prosperity and well-being.

These three elements complicate the situation but can also contribute to its solution and guarantee stability and sustainability to any just solution agreed upon by the parties.

14: How to Get There

This book started as an intellectual exercise to see if it is possible to have a vision for a solution that addresses the main interests of both parties, without endorsing their respective ideologies. Showing that a two-state solution is no longer a possible answer to that question, I embarked upon this project, not to provide a political platform much less to start a political party or movement. However, as the vision began to take shape, I had to deal with the serious question of how to achieve such a solution, or risk its being dismissed as merely a pipe dream.

Fundamental Obstacles
To answer this question, we have to deal with a number of fundamental obstacles that are currently blocking not just this vision, but any hope for a peaceful solution:

The Holocaust Syndrome. There is no denial that the Jewish people have suffered a momentous trauma of genocide, coming as the culmination of millennia of antisemitic discrimination and hatred, which has deeply scarred their collective soul. This trauma has given power and authority to a jaundiced view of politics which is often exploited by cynical politicians. According to this view, human nature is evil, international law is meaningless, public opinion is fickle, and only brute and overwhelming force stands between the Jewish people and another holocaust. The conclusion is that Jews can rely on nothing and no one other than their own military strength. The trauma is indeed so powerful, that even when military strength is abundantly available in abundance it is never seen as sufficient. Furthermore, serious attempts at peace are viewed either with skepticism as to their motives or are dismissed as hopelessly naïve.

As a result of this view, even genuine peaceful gestures by potential opponents are viewed with great suspicion, skepticism and fear. In addition, the slightest disagreement with their policies or opposition to their interests is seen as part of the indescribable evil of antisemitism. It is treated as a harbinger of dire consequences, which needs to be massively attacked, lest it lead to a repeat of the Holocaust.

The fact that the Holocaust occurred in the heart of enlightened Europe, where Jews appeared to be successfully assimilated only strengthens that fear beyond the point where rational discussion is possible or realistic appraisal of the situation is meaningful. Unless and until that trauma is healed and ameliorated, even the most ideal solution will be impossible to realize. Security will never be achieved, but will remain an ever-present factor, not only guiding the policies of Israel, but also justifying any and all actions on its behalf.

One of the ways to begin to deal with this factor is to be vigilant and clear in our opposition to antisemitism. It also means, however, putting it into perspective, in the context of opposition to all forms of racism and discrimination, and refusing to trivialize it by demonizing every opposition to Israeli policies as antisemitic. Unfortunately, repeated pronouncements of understanding Israel's "security needs" and demanding that any peace moves should ensure and guarantee Israel's security, often inadvertently reinforce this Holocaust syndrome rather than heal it.

The Imbalance of Power between the Two Parties. Jewish Israelis today are immeasurably more powerful than Palestinian Arabs. On the ground, they hold all of the land of Israel/Palestine and control all points of entry and exit from it. They are economically and technologically superior. (Israel enjoys a per capita GDP of $42,000, compared to only $3000 for West Bank/Gaza). Militarily, they hold overwhelming dominance over Palestinians and all their potential allies combined. They also have nuclear, WMD weapons, and an indigenous arms industry that is one of the leading exporters of weapons in the world. They are world-class leaders in innovation in drone and smart bomb technology. On top of all that, they enjoy the practical and material support of the world's only superpower, which is committed to maintaining their qualitative edge over all their potential enemies. They have the ability to project their power, both military and economic, far beyond their borders.

The Palestinians, by contrast, are in a much weaker position. They are economically, militarily and technologically inferior to Israelis. They are also fragmented, geographically separated from each other, suffering from poor leadership, which is ineffective at best, and collaborationist with Israel at worst. The power discrepancy cannot possibly be greater.

No privileged group ever willingly gives up its privileges, unless it meets substantial internal and external pressures. Throughout the world, demands for equality appear as oppression to privileged groups. No progress towards a more just solution which requires any sacrifices or abandonment of privilege can come about until the power imbalance is addressed. The traumatic syndrome described above, however, makes all actions to reduce the power imbalance difficult, as they could inadvertently entrench the feeling of persecution and insecurity embedded in the Holocaust syndrome.

To move forward, therefore, is a challenge which requires hard choices, dedicated action, and a long struggle. It is only hoped that the vision described in this book provides justification that such struggle is indeed worth engaging in, and that such a struggle can be carried out by people of goodwill committed to justice and the ultimate good of both parties, rather than as a partisan exercise that favors only one party at the expense of the other.

Paucity of Joint Actions. Since the Oslo process, there has been a marked reduction of joint actions and contacts between Israelis and Palestinians. Some of this was the result of a deliberate ideology of *hafrada* (separation) pursued by the Israeli government. This was enforced by building the Separation Wall, checkpoints, and various military regulations. It has also been encouraged by failure of peace activists on both sides to make joint activities a priority. The Palestinian Authority encouraged this trend by insisting on its status as the only legitimate interlocutor to Israel and discouraging direct contacts between Palestinian and Israeli activists. Israeli Jewish activists felt they were somehow supporting Palestinian statehood by staying away with the understanding that "we are here and they are there," and letting Palestinians forge ahead on their own. This was a tragic error.

Palestinian activists have also contributed to this failure. They wisely opted for nonviolent resistance, which included BDS (Boycotts, Divestment and Sanctions). In boycotting Israeli structures and institutions, they gave too much weight to their "anti-normalization" campaign. They reduced their contacts and cooperation with Israeli Jewish peace activists in order to avoid appearances of "normalization" and acceptance of a very unacceptable situation. The slogan "co-resistance, not coexistence" was honored more in the negative (avoidance of joint actions that are not sufficiently pure) than in the positive (seeking joint activities wherever possible). As a result, each community was left largely to seek its struggle separately and the joint struggle against occupation and racist domination suffered accordingly. As we recognize the failure of the two-state solution, and the need for a new vision of a joint life and a joint future, we should seek to maximize, not minimize joint contacts and activities. At the same time, we need to be conscious of the need to avoid the appeal of "normalization" and acceptance of an unacceptable status quo or working within the parameters dictated by an unjust situation in the name of realism.

Action Program toward a One State Solution
The essence of my approach has been to seek a new vision that meets the minimum requirements of each community without negating the interest of the other. If we follow this approach, we could also come up with an action program that meets those same needs. An activist program embodying these principles may include the following:

Reevaluate our Outlook towards Settlers and Hamas. As the numbers of settlers reaches close to 800,000 and the Green Line becomes slowly erased, Palestinians need to rethink their attitudes towards some of the settlers, who often resemble a cross section of Israeli society, and not just its extremists. For many years, the two-state solution required demonizing all settlers while accepting Israeli Zionists who lived in pre-1967 borders. It may be time to rethink this paradigm. A tiny minority of settlers can even be seen as reasonable and sympathetic to coexistence with Palestinians, while the minority of Israelis inclined to peace continues to shrink. I even met one settler rabbi who believed in full genuine equality between Jews and Palestinians in all of historic Palestine, as well as in the Palestinian Right of Return, which is more than I can say for most Israeli "leftists." A joint future requires that blanket demonization of all settlers be reexamined.

Similarly, the blanket demonization of Hamas needs to be radically reexamined by Israelis. Hamas represents a large sector of the Palestinian population and contains many moderates who should be brought into the conversation. As we contemplate a joint future for both communities, we must find ways to involve settlers as well as Hamas in the conversation.

End the siege of Gaza and allow freedom of people and goods into and out of the Strip. The siege was initially undertaken as a political move to punish Gazans for their support of Hamas and to prevent continuity between the West Bank and Gaza. It was deliberately used as a measure to fragment Palestinians and prevent Palestinian statehood, but it cannot be allowed to remain as a permanent feature of life. With due consideration for the desire to prevent weapons from entering Gaza (a failed exercise in all cases) draconian controls over the civilian life and economy of two million souls in the Gaza strip cannot be a permanent state of affairs. It must end. The puny efforts of some in Gaza to militarily resist Israel are strategically insignificant, and in any case, cannot be completely deterred by force alone. But given the relative quiet (from Gaza's side) the siege must be lifted. This is something all parties must work on NOW.

Palestinians Abandon Armed Resistance. Armed struggle is never an end in and of itself. It is only a method for achieving political ends which seem to be elusive now. However deeply oppressed, and however justly provoked Palestinians are, armed resistance cannot help them in their present situation. No political or national goal can be advanced by acts of desperation, especially if aimed at the civilian "softer targets." To the contrary, they are definitely bound to be counterproductive. The issue is not legitimacy of armed resistance, which is in fact legitimate and recognized by international law, but its efficacy. We Palestinians will do well (from our own perspective) to suspend any such actions. The emotional rush or satisfaction of "doing something," or "making the other side suffer", or even as a measure to force Israelis or the rest of the world to remember that we exist, are not sufficient reasons to do things that are counterproductive to our cause.

Israel Chooses Peaceful Means to Deal with Palestinians. By the same token, Israeli continued reliance on the army and deadly force has also proven ineffective and "deterrence" has not worked. New thinking is required by Israelis to reexamine the efficacy of reliance on military power as the preferred tool of dealing with Palestinians.

Call for New Palestinian Elections. The existing leadership both in Hamas and Fatah have failed their people miserably. New elections can only help by bringing new individuals into leadership positions both of these two parties and of the Palestinian people.

Expand Language Education. Introducing the teaching of Hebrew as a third language in Palestinian schools, and Arabic as a third language in Israeli schools should be a priority for both sides.

Intensify the Struggle against Collective Punishment and Administrative Measures. Many of the forms of control used by Israel against Palestinians attempt to fashion the behavior of the entire Palestinian community by punishing members of that community and rendering them all subject to the arbitrary acts of Israel. Such actions contravene international law, common morality, and basic human decency. Some would say they also contravene the character and morality of Judaism and of the nature of society Jews wish to have for Israel. Such measures may find some justification in times of crisis but cannot serve as a permanent feature of any peoples' existence.

Take Joint Actions towards a Just Peace. While activists may not always agree on the final desired outcome, yet they generally have a long list of targets that they can jointly work against. More efforts should be undertaken to create joint activities that forcefully confront the occupation and the ongoing injustices while holding the vision of a joint future for both sides. This is a particularly difficult task where Gazans are concerned since the siege effectively bans contacts and therefore joint activities with Gazans.

Israeli Action Program toward a One-State Solution
Israel, as the stronger party, should also be pressured to unilaterally take a number of steps that ameliorate the current situation and provide possibilities for a better future. Each of these actions would be a step in the right direction, and can be undertaken with minimal security risks, and without necessarily prejudicing the eventual outcome:

End all administrative detentions and release all administrative detainees.

Remove all restrictions on normal movement of goods and services between the West Bank and Israel, as well as between Gaza and the West Bank. Specific individuals may still be prevented from movement into Israel by court decree, upon good cause, but the blanket prohibitions must be lifted, especially with respect to access to East Jerusalem. This has actually been tried a number of times, with good results. The continued restrictions have a political, not security basis.

Remove all barriers, checkpoints and obstructions <u>within</u> the West Bank and allow freedom of movement for goods and persons. These restrictions currently hamper economic development, create daily humiliations and bedevilment, and their contribution to Israel's security is negligible. Their continued presence has a great negative impact on the lives of Palestinians and their contribution to increasing hatred and enmity is enormous.

Grant Palestinians permission to build in Area C of the West Bank and turn over zoning and planning authority in those areas to them.

Create new legislative and constitutional guarantees for equality inside Israel itself, and making the promise of equality in Israel's Declaration of Independence operational and binding. This means reversing the current wave of laws and regulations, including the Nation-state law, and embarking on a different tack with respect to genuine equality for Palestinians who are Israeli citizens.

Make all residents of the West Bank, including Jewish settlers, subject to the same laws, administered by civil, not military courts. This measure does not need Palestinian approval. Those Jewish settlers who wish to continue to live illegally in the West Bank, for whatever reason, must be required as a minimum to pay the price of living in equality with Palestinians in that area. Such a step could take the form of extending certain Israeli privileges to West Bank Palestinians or alleviating certain burdens from the Arab population that would be intolerable to Jewish settlers. Either way, it would promote equality without prejudicing Israeli security or the eventual political outcome.

☙

It may be argued that all these suggestions only beautify and prolong the occupation rather than remove it. My answer is that each and every one of these suggestions can be pursued without abandoning one's own political beliefs or one's own struggle for the ultimate political outcome. They may not lead to the vision I have outlined, but they are certainly steps in the right direction, and should be undertaken by people of goodwill, even if they do not accept my vision for a solution. They attempt to address the current intolerable situation which has been oppressing the local population for half a century while pretending to be temporary.

I firmly believe that it is the fate of both Israelis Jews and Palestinian Arabs to live together in this land. Neither side, with all the outside help it can muster, will be able to eliminate the other. The outcome should not be perpetual conflict and bloodshed, with each side viewing the other as an existential threat, in a zero-sum paradigm that has been the main feature of this conflict. A better vision exists whereby a different future can await both of us. A vision for a state that meets the deepest need of each group, and that yields a more vibrant, rich, and beneficial society for each community that can be a shining example for others in the area and throughout the world. The details may differ, but such a view based on empathy and understanding of the other rather than negating and demonizing them is a far worthier object to pursue. I dare to imagine that it can lead to a richer, more vibrant Palestinian Nationalism, and to a more humane, moral, and richer Zionist movement.

Executive Summary

It is now commonly acknowledged that the two-state solution is physically impossible to implement. The premise of the Two States Solution (two-state solution) was that the 1967 War provided an opportunity for a pragmatic compromise between the Zionist movement in the State of Israel, and the Palestinian national movement with its Arab allies. This could be achieved in a strategic "land for peace" formula whereby the state of Israel would withdraw from the lands it recently occupied, in return for peace and normalization. Additional elements were sometimes mentioned such as: sharing East Jerusalem, a Palestinian Right of Return to the new Palestinian state, as well as security arrangements such as the demilitarization of the State of Palestine. Clearly, Jewish settlements would run counter to this proposed compromise.

Now, in 2021, the extent, depth, and longevity of the occupation has created new facts on the ground, notably the colonization of the West Bank with roughly 700,000 settlers, with their entire legal, administrative, political, transportation, security and economic infrastructure. The changes are so profound that they render the proposed compromise (two-state solution) no longer possible, even if Israel and the Palestinians were fully committed to it. The recent announcement of the Trump Plan, as well as steps towards annexation of portions of the West Bank further make this compromise no longer a viable possibility.

But if that is the case, what is the alternative? What is the endgame for those on both sides, as well as their supporters outside and the international community itself? Some out-of-the box thinking is required: a new strategy by which we may pursue peace, justice, some measure of stability, and an end to the conflict. Such new thinking would require a radical reformulation of the language, assumptions, and orientation of people on all sides. How to achieve it is a totally different question.

Why Two-State Solution Thinking Persists

But before we approach this Herculean task, we must understand why two-state solution thinking persists and continues to dominate the discussion, even in the face of a current reality, that thoughtful analysts agree is no longer viable. There are a number of reasons why that must be understood, since they constitute a serious hurdle to any new and innovative thinking.

1. The compromise was eminently reasonable at the time it was suggested. It reflected both the balance of power at the time, and the majority interests of both protagonists. It was vehemently condemned by sizable populations on both sides, but slowly gained majority support, and became the official platform of both communities. It did not require the repudiation or radical rethinking of any of the ideologies involved, but merely limited the application of such ideologies to geographic portions of the contested land.

2. International law supported the two-state solution in that it prohibited the acquisition of land through armed conflict. It proclaimed the status of the territories in question to be "occupied" under the law of belligerent occupation. Even the Israeli High Court supported this legal classification and does so to this day. This was also reflected in numerous pronouncements of the UN Security Council and was affirmed unanimously by the International Court of Justice in the case of the Wall, 15 - 0. The single dissenting judge in that case agreed with the rest of the judges on the matter of the status of the occupied territories and the applicability of the Fourth Geneva Convention to them.

3. This is the position of all the countries of the world, including the United States, and was reaffirmed by the Saudi Initiative, which promised full normalization with all the Arab and Moslem countries in return for full Israeli withdrawal from lands occupied in 1967.

4. The alternative to the two-state solution, some form of a one-state solution (one person-one vote), was viewed by many as a repudiation of Zionism, a rejection and a call for the destruction of the concept of a Jewish state. In the minds of many, this was akin to calling for expulsion of Jews from Palestine, and possibly a second Holocaust. The prospect was so unthinkable that in many venues no serious discussion of a one-state solution was even tolerated.

5. Ending the occupation. Pro-Palestinian activists (and their Arab and international supporters) gradually changed their goal from the "liberation of Palestine" to "ending the occupation." This was a slogan and program acceptable to many international activists, who cared about peace and justice, but who were reluctant to take positions that were perceived as anti-Israeli. The presence of a sizable 'peace movement' inside Israel that claimed to support the two-state solution contributed to this.

6. Deception. It is possible that many in the consecutive Israeli governments since 1967 never believed in the two-state solution and were deceiving the world, as well as their own public, by claiming they supported a two-state solution while working hard to undermine it at every level.

7. The fly in the ointment of the two-state solution was the settler project, and the settlers themselves. This project introduced hundreds of thousands of Jewish settlers into the occupied territories, while still claiming the privileges of Israeli citizenship for them. This directly contradicted the entire logic of the proposed compromise. In effect it championed Zionist dominion over all the contested area of Palestine. Each additional settler, or confiscation of a dunam for settlements, or creation of structures, including roads, courts, laws, regulations, called into serious question the claims of Israeli governments concerning their support of a two-state solution. Rather, their actions reaffirmed Zionist claims to all of Palestine for the Jewish people. Therefore, a genuine support of two-state solution required opposition to the settlement enterprise.

8. The two-state solution has become a mirage which permits the status quo of settlement expansion to continue. Failure to achieve the two-state solution could be blamed on the absence of effective Palestinian leadership, lack of unity among Palestinians, or lack of sufficient outside pressure. Modifications to the two-state solution are proposed, such as designation of "settlement blocks," exchange of territories, and endless negotiations. Meanwhile Israeli Zionist control of the occupied territories continues to thrive and expand. Even the Oslo Process and the creation of the Palestinian Authority did not change this formula. Inertia is a powerful force. It is no wonder that Israeli politicians, and even AIPAC itself, claim to support the two-state solution while effectively ensuring it will never be implemented.

New Thinking is Necessary
To think out of the box regarding a future for Israeli Jews and their supporters, and for Palestinian Arabs and their supporters,

we must start by acknowledging that the ideologies of the two protagonists are basically incompatible: One ideology wanted to have a Jewish state in the land (whether by divine right, or historical connection, or existential need) which serves the interest of all Jews worldwide, and is dedicated exclusively to their interests. This necessarily requires the elimination, subjugation, and repression of the indigenous non-Jewish population. On the other hand, a different ideology insists on an Arab Palestine as part of the Arab world, treats all Jews—other than the original Palestinian Jews—as foreign invaders with no rights and connection to the Land. Such an ideology logically requires the elimination or forced expulsion of most Israelis as recent immigrants, and denies Jewish religious and cultural aspirations and requirements.

New thinking, beyond the two-state solution, would require each group to sufficiently empathize with and understand the hopes, fears, interests, and aspirations of the other group. It would lead each group to sufficiently moderate/alter, and otherwise change its own ideology to accommodate the other group rather than vanquish and dominate it and deny it any legitimacy.

To achieve this outcome, we need to ask Zionists, "What do you really want? What are your rock bottom needs, and can those needs be accommodated in Palestine/Israel without thoroughly negating the interests and reality of the Palestinians?" We also need to ask the Palestinians, "What is it that you really want? What are your rock bottom needs? Can these needs be accommodated in a state where you are not dominant, and where Israeli Jews are roughly equal in number to the Palestinian Arabs?"

Implicit in both questions is a belief that while an electoral democracy requires one-person one-vote, a state that belongs to more than one major ethnic/religious group cannot afford to ignore the other. It must find a formula that accommodates all of them and contains sufficient iron-clad legal and institutional guarantees that protects each group, particularly the minority against the caprice of the majority. This is especially true where historic differences and recent enmities shape present realities. New structures must be created, and iron-clad guarantees must be firmly established in constitutions and laws that cannot be altered or overturned by numerical majorities, or that require a supermajority of more than one house of representatives, so as to prevent them from being derailed by the group which has a numerical majority.

In our situation, the system requires—in addition to internal legal and other controls—a high level of international support, guarantees, and legitimacy in light of the extensive interest of and involvement of significant outside actors. Specifically, the religious importance of the Land to all three monotheistic religions, and particularly Jerusalem, gives the international community a significant stake. It is of interest to ensure the governance of the whole country in a manner that guarantees open access to it, and non-exclusive control over its destiny. Jewish or Moslem claims of exclusivity cannot be tolerated. Thank God, since the times of the Crusaders, Christians have ceased to make such exclusive religious claims.

For a solution to commend itself to people of goodwill on both sides, and significant third parties as well, it must address the major needs of each community. These needs should be identified by each side as bottom-line irreducible requirements, as opposed to desired or demanded outcomes. These needs must be met and addressed by the new order regardless of whether either group is in the numeric majority or minority now or in the future. We suggest possible bottom-line irreducible requirements may be similar to the following nine points.

Essential Elements of the New Order
1. Right of Return. Jews have insisted on a Right of Return to Israel as a fundamental right for any and every Jew throughout the world, particularly if they feel persecuted or endangered for their Jewishness. As it stands now, this right is not qualified by the need to show persecution or fear of a tangible threat. The institutions of the State actively promote *aliyah* and incentivize Jews to come to Palestine. The availability of this right is a serious requirement for Zionists which Palestinians must accept. On the other hand, Palestinians, who have been forcibly denied access to their homeland, also must have a recognized right of return (*awdah*).

2. Equality and Non-discrimination. The State of Israel has failed in law and in practice to provide even to its own Arab citizens full and true equality. Palestinians will require the new state—which is likely to continue in the foreseeable future to be dominated by Jews for a number of reasons—to strictly abide by the principle of equality in the public sphere. Public institutions, lands, funds, and resources must be utilized in the interest of all citizens, and discrimination must not be tolerated. Arabic, which is currently formally recognized as an official language in Israel, will need to be deliberately incorporated into public life, on a par with Hebrew. While it was a Zionist need to promote Hebrew in Israel, and indeed to revive it after centuries of non-use, there can be no excuse for the deliberate downgrading of Arabic. Currently, Arabic signs, where they exist even in the West Bank appear to be deliberately misspelt, and it is easier to find government documents in Amharic (the language of the recent Ethiopian immigrants) than in Arabic.

3. Freedom of Movement. Freedom of movement within the new state must be guaranteed. Restrictions of travel between the West Bank, Gaza, the settlements, Jerusalem and pre '67 Israel must be removed, as well as the Wall and the checkpoints. Discretionary restrictions on travel within as well as to and from the new state must be removed.

4. Relations with the Arab world. Israeli Jews feel a great connection to diaspora Jews and obtain a lot of support from them, and advocate that such Jews have a stake in Israel as well as a responsibility for it. Similarly, Palestinian Arabs feel they are an integral part of the Arab world and get—or at least expect—support from them. The new state will have to deal with both these inclinations. In this sense, Palestinians need to reevaluate their pan-Arab identity, and adjust it to reflect the reality that their state now is both Jewish and Arab to its very core.

5. Defense. For a number of reasons, primarily the trauma of the Holocaust and the bitter experience of anti-Jewish antisemitism in the West, Israelis have a heightened sensitivity to control of the army. The new State may require that the Minister of Defense, as well as a majority of the top brass in the army be Jewish as a matter of permanent constitutional law. Palestinians, however, must be free to join the army on the basis of equality, while all citizens who wish, must be free to demand exemption from military service for reasons of conscience.

6. Legal Protections. In addition to a constitution that embodies strict guarantees that safeguard the interest of either group, the "Protection Clauses" must be safeguarded from alteration by requiring that they can only be altered by high majorities. It must also be cleared by a super majority (four out of five) of a special constitutional court where each group has at least two representatives. In other significant ministries and public bodies, quotas must dictate the minimum number of representatives at the highest level, while all other positions are filled on a merit, and non-discriminatory basis. In government ministries, the deputy for each Ministry must belong to the other major group. In this manner the fear that a high-level public servant who belongs to one group will be oppressive to those in the minority group will be eliminated. This and other similar "Protection Clauses" will remove the 'demographic threat' and ensure that a group which has numerical majority will not be able to oppress a numerical minority, or that a future change in the numerical balance between the two communities will not make the minority vulnerable to oppression by the majority.

7. Ministry of Cooperation and Coexistence. Recognizing that the security of citizens is a vital interest of the country, and in appreciation for the past experience of both peoples, the country shall invest at least 10% of its defense budget into deliberate activities by a governmental ministry of tolerance that will promote understanding of the history, culture and language of each community by the other. It will also promote joint activities and programs intended to heal the hurts of the past and build understanding and tolerance between the two communities.

8. Civil Law. While personal status matters are currently handled by the religious courts of the different communities, new civil laws must be promulgated that will ensure the rights of secular individuals, mixed couples, and religious communities that are not currently recognized. These include Reform and Conservative

Jews, as well as Evangelicals. Without derogation from the existing rights of religious courts, individuals who choose not to be so governed should be allowed to follow their conscience and not be forced to submit to religious courts of their particular religious community. This system could be a model for other nations in the Middle East which are currently governed by the Ottoman Millet System.

9. Name, Character, Public Holidays, Symbols and Flag. Careful thought and creativity with input from both sides are required to have these elements of national identity reflect the desires of both communities without exclusivity or discrimination against the others.

ଔ

Finally, concrete steps must be jointly undertaken by each community to advance the possibility of realizing this vision. These steps can be initiated now, and do not require prior commitment to a specific outcome nor do they preclude any particular ideology. They require a rethinking of the positions of settlers and Hamas as partners in the peace process, as well as joint activities towards ending the most outrageous forms of oppression. Ultimately, they require rethinking Zionism and Palestinian nationalism altogether.

Jonathan Kuttab is a co-founder of the Palestinian human rights group Al-Haq and co-founder of Nonviolence International. A well-known international human rights attorney, he has practiced in the US, Palestine and Israel. He serves on the Board of Bethlehem Bible College and is President of the Board of Holy Land Trust. He was the head of the Legal Committee negotiating the Cairo Agreement of 1994 between Israel and the PLO. He is a co-founder and board member of Just Peace Advocates, a Canadian-based human rights organization.

For more information about Jonathan Kuttab, please go to jonathankuttab.org

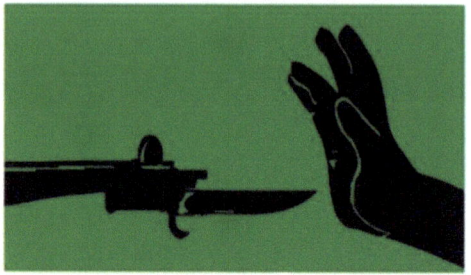

NONVIOLENCE INTERNATIONAL

Nonviolence International advocates for active nonviolence and supports creative campaigns worldwide. We serve as a backbone organization of the nonviolent movement and provide fiscal sponsorship to partners all over the globe. We share transformative stories of dynamic nonviolent movements that give us hope in difficult times and reshape what we view as possible. By sharing these inspirational stories and supporting these movements we help to create a peaceful and just future.

Organizational Information. Nonviolence International (NVI) was co-founded by Palestinian activists Jonathan Kuttab and Mubarak Awad in 1989. NVI is a 501(c)(3) organization registered in Washington, DC, USA. NVI is also a non-governmental organization in Special Consultative Status with the Economic and Social Council of the United Nations.

To order a paper copy or to find out more please contact Nonviolence International at:
https://www.nonviolenceinternational.net/beyond2states

If this book has inspired you, please visit our website for action steps, resources and more.
https://www.nonviolenceinternational.net/

Nonviolence International is the fiscal sponsor for the following outstanding organizations working for peace and justice in Palestine and Israel.

US Boat to Gaza is a part of the Freedom Flotilla Coalition, which sends boats to Gaza in an effort to end the blockade.
https://www.nonviolenceinternational.net/ffc_freedom_flotilla_coalition

The Hebron International Resource Network (**HIRN**)**,** founded in 201, works to support Palestinians living near illegal settlements. HIRN advocates for clean water, access to electricity, safe housing, education, free movement, and other resources.
https://www.nonviolenceinternational.net/hirn_partner

Holy Land Trust (HLT) is a Palestinian nonprofit organization that seeks to empower Palestinian communities and aid them in resistance to oppression.
https://www.nonviolenceinternational.net/holy_land_trust_partner

The Center for Jewish Nonviolence (CJNV) is an international network that strengthens co-resistance in Israeli-Palestinian solidarity. CJNV seeks a just and equitable end to the occupation. https://www.nonviolenceinternational.net/cjnv_partner

Just Peace Advocates is a Canadian based independent human rights organization promoting Just Peace/Paix Juste through the rule of law and respect for human rights in Canada and around the world particularly for the Palestinian and Kashmiri peoples. NVI has a partnership with JPA and Jonathan Kuttab is a board member and co-founder. https://www.justpeaceadvocates.ca

We Are Not Numbers, based in Gaza, shares and celebrates stories by young people, with experienced global English language authors mentoring the youth. https://wearenotnumbers.org

The following new fiscal partners work globally and will also work in Palestine and Israel.

Solidarity 2020 and Beyond is a global network of activists, trainers, and organizers that provides support and solidarity for grassroots activists around the world utilizing strategic nonviolent action to build campaigns and movements for change.
https://solidarity2020andbeyond.org

Norm-creative SETTINGS, a Swedish-based group, has developed an activist app called Micro Action Movement (M.A.M.) to encourage and support discrete actions by people or entities that can be easily replicated to promote nonviolent social change. It brings everyday people, artists and civil society together in suggesting and participating in everyday micro actions.
https://www.facebook.com/MicroActionMovement

Stay connected with us through our website
https://www.nonviolenceinternational.net/

and our social media!
Youtube: https://www.youtube.com/nonviolence
Twitter: https://twitter.com/NVInt
Facebook: https://www.facebook.com/NonviolenceInternational/

Publishing in early 2021…

Civil Resistance Tactics of the 21st Century

Nonviolence International is excited to announce a groundbreaking monograph *Civil Resistance Tactics of the 21st Century* written by our Director, Michael Beer. Published by the International Center for Nonviolent Conflict, the monograph catalogues 346 tactics of nonviolent action. It builds upon the foundational work, *The Politics of Nonviolent Action,* by noted activist and scholar Gene Sharp. We are profoundly grateful for Gene Sharp's endorsement of this new work.

NVI has been collecting tactics for 10 years and hosts an interactive database at tactics.nonviolenceinternational.net.

Civil Resistance Tactics of the 21st Century includes an extensive discussion of the elements, practice, classification, and organization of nonviolent action. Following this overview, each of the 346 tactics are described in concise though sufficient detail for both practitioners and students of nonviolence.

Among the monograph's 346 tactical examples are digital games, outing, cacalerozas, die-ins, citizen inspections, divestment, and marriage inclusion.

We are grateful for the many tactics documented by other scholars that are included in this work. The monograph also documents scores of previously unrecognized tactics and proposes a new categorization of nonviolent action.

Each tactic offers insight into people's perseverance and resilience in the face of repression, demonstrating not only the drive to fight for rights, freedom, and justice, but also the opportunity to be innovative and adaptive in leading resistance struggles.

This monograph will serve as a basic text not only "in the field" of action, but also in classrooms studying nonviolence, protest and resistance, peace building, and conflict resolution around the world.

The monograph will be available in eBook and print editions.